# GEMSTONES
# TO
# JEWELLERY

Printed by The Continental Printing Company
Limited, Hong Kong

# GEMSTONES
# TO
# JEWELLERY

EDITED BY

BILL JAMES

MURRAY

SYDNEY        MELBOURNE

First published 1967, by
THE K. G. MURRAY PUBLISHING
COMPANY PTY LTD
142 Clarence Street, Sydney

# CONTENTS

# ILLUSTRATIONS

# ACKNOWLEDGMENTS

MY MOST SINCERE THANKS are due to my wife Dorothy for her encouragement and practical help without which this book would never have been accomplished. Others who played a most important part behind the scenes were Mr. and Mrs. Harvey Kerslake of Artarmon, N.S.W., Mrs. Enid Ashelford of Bathurst, N.S.W., Mr. Allan Ireland of Broken Hill, N.S.W. and Mrs. Elizabeth Fry of Burwood, Vic.

Most of the excellent pictures are due to the skill of Mr. Walter Kavanagh.

BILL JAMES

# INTRODUCTION

THIS BOOK IS FOR THOSE who collect gemstones from nature and for those who buy their gemstones, for it starts from the moment when the gem rough arrives on the workbench. It is also a controversial book because it caters both for those who buy part of their jewellery ready-made in the form of settings and those who insist that all parts of jewellery should be hand-made.

Nowadays the gemstone hobby is reaching out beyond merely cutting cabochons, beautiful as they can be. Hobby gemworkers want to turn their stones into articles of lasting value that can be worn and used and admired.

There are two ways in which that can be done. One is by buying ready-made findings and settings from the lapidary supply shops. The other is by adding the knowledge of how to make jewellery to the lapidary hobby. This book goes into both alternatives with expert advice and tuition.

Until fairly recently, some of the ready-made settings offered to hobby gemworkers were ugly, clumsy and decidedly cheap-looking. Settings of this description vulgarised the lovely natural gems mounted in them.

However, as illustrations in this book make it clear, it is now possible to buy elegant and exquisite settings in solid silver and gold plate. Using settings of this quality jewellery can be home-made that has the professional look.

No longer is the hobby worker tied to cutting cabochons. Modern mechanical faceting heads of the type described in this book make it possible for anyone to facet their own gems. The ability to carry out a series of instructions, none of which are unduly difficult, is all that is needed to cut brilliants.

Jewellery-made-easy does not please everyone, however. Some people feel that a hobby should be difficult enough to be a challenge to the skill and patience of those engaged in it. Jewellery-making that consists of cementing stones into ready-made bought settings is not jewellery-making at all, they contend.

As Laurel Gorn, the prominent Sydney jewellery teacher who is a major collaborator in this book, puts it: "With a little practice in silver soldering and a knowledge of the precious metals, anyone can buy cast pieces and put them together to form a finished piece of jewellery, but this is not handcraft and no genuine artist-craftsman will use this method."

Mrs. Gorn of Dee Why, N.S.W., has been active in both the lapidary and jewellery hobbies for more than seven years. She was one of the founders of the Parramatta Lapidary Club in 1960 and also taught jewellery-making at the Parramatta Evening College in that year. Later she also taught at the Eastwood Evening College.

A Sydney professional jeweller had taught Mrs. Gorn in the 1950s and at that time she joined the New South Wales Society of Arts and Crafts. She twice won the Society's Soderberg Memorial Prize in 1960-61. In 1965 she shared the second prize at the Mosman exhibition of the Arts Council of Australia. Two years ago she helped to found the Northside Gem Club.

Other well-known teachers who have collaborated in this book are Jack S. Taylor, of St. Leonards, N.S.W., and Lloyd Meller, of Epping, N.S.W. Mr. Taylor represents the third generation of a Sydney jewellery family. He was a founder member of the Gemmological Association of Australia which awarded its first diploma to him in 1947 and five years later he founded the Lapidary Club of New South Wales to launch Australia's organised lapidary hobby.

Six years ago when Mr. Taylor was teaching at Eastwood Evening College, one of his most promising students was Lloyd Meller. Four years ago Mr. Meller took over the class. In an informed chapter of this book he tells the secrets of cutting top quality cabochons.

As a footnote to most of the chapters, readers will find a resume of the cost of the articles mentioned as at October, 1966. These prices are given only for the purposes of information and interest. Many people like to estimate what it will cost them to take up a new hobby. Although the prices quoted here are subject to fluctuation, they will be accurate enough to act as a guide for some time to come.

# 1

# EARLIEST OF JEWELS

ATTRACTIVE, BRIGHT WATERWORN PEBBLES were mankind's first jewels and lapidary art, as the fashioning of gemstones is properly called, began with polishing these natural rounded shapes.

One of the most famous of these stones was the Black Prince's Ruby, a red spinel the size of a small hen's egg. In 1367, when Pedro the Cruel, King of Castile, gave this jewel to the English prince, polishing was the most that lapidaries of the time could do to show off its beauty.

Today the big balas ruby blazes in the Imperial State Crown of the British regalia. It still displays a shape carved over countless centuries by fire and frost, wind-blown sand and rushing water. It has survived amazing adventures. In 1415 it was in the crown that saved Henry V of England from a sword blow at the battle of Agincourt. In 1671 it was found in the pocket of one of the thieves who tried to steal the Crown Jewels from the Tower of London.

*The Black Prince's Ruby, the size of a small hen's egg, as it is set in the Imperial State Crown of the British regalia.*

But 600 years are next to nothing in the story of a gemstone. Perhaps the greatest romance of our jewels and certainly the one least realised is that many of them were produced long ago while our world was still in the final convulsions of creation. Gemstones were by-products of the forces that shaped continents and raised mountains. Something of these wonders can still be seen and felt in them.

Gemstones in their natural shape are known as baroques. As their introduction to lapidary art, hobby gemworkers throughout Australia are converting these stones to attractive costume jewellery with the aid of bought metal accessories known as findings. These consist of chains, clasps, pins, bars and so on. The gems range from amethysts and opals to beach pebbles. Like the Black Prince's Ruby, these stones are merely smoothed and polished but nowadays this is done with the aid of scientific abrasives and electrically-powered tumbling machines, which can do in days what once took weeks of patient work.

Baroque stones were never enough to satisfy the true lapidary. Men soon discovered that the shapes of gemstones could be changed by rubbing them with harder substances. Thousands of years ago the Greeks were carving likenesses of gods, kings and heroes as intaglios and cameos. The artistry of some of this early work has never been excelled.

Roman lapidaries produced another style of gem. These stones were ground and polished into an oval, domed shape that gained the name of cabochons, from the French word for a bald head. This smooth rounded shape is the best for displaying the colours and markings of opaque and translucent stones. It also happens to be the best shape for resisting wear, a fact which makes it ideal for softer materials.

The hardness of gemstones, like that of other minerals and related substances, is measured according to a scale devised by an 18th century German mineralogist named Frederick Mohs. Mohs' scale took talc as the softest mineral and a diamond as the hardest, ranging eight other minerals between in an ascending scale. This is Mohs' scale: **1**, talc; **2**, gypsum (selenite); **3**, calcite; **4**, fluorite; **5**, apatite; **6**, orthoclase feldspar; **7**, quartz; **8**, topaz; **9**, corundum (sapphire); **10**, diamond.

This scale is somewhat arbitrary and the difference in hardness between the minerals given as examples is not the same in every case. But the important point is that each mineral in the scale is hard enough to scratch the surface of every mineral below it. By using these minerals named as standards it is also possible to decide the relative hardness of other substances—a finger-nail is about hardness 2 for instance, and one of our bronze cents hardness 3, while the steel blade of a knife is hardness 6.

As a further example, let us take a piece of aragonite, which has a similar chemical composition to calcite. The hardness of this mineral is inclined to vary, but the hardest sort of aragonite will scratch calcite. It will not scratch fluorite, however, and is only faintly scratched by it. So the hardness of this particular piece of aragonite must be almost 4.

Any gemstone of hardness 4 that is worn constantly will be quickly disfigured. That is ensured by the hardness of quartz which Mohs rates as 7. Quartz is one of the most common and widespread substances on earth. It makes up the gritty part of all the world's dust. Exposed to this grit, the polished surface of any gemstone of less than hardness 7 is eventually worn dull, although the scratches are less obvious on the curved surface of a cabochon. For this reason, with rare exceptions, stones below hardness 7 are cut and polished as cabochons.

Two other factors govern the use of relatively soft gemstones in jewellery—how often the stones are worn and the way in which they are worn. Occasional use combined with careful storage will keep a stone beautiful for many years that could otherwise be ruined in months. The beauty of the softer stones can also be prolonged by the use made of them in jewellery. A cabochon of aragonite would retain its pleasing appearance far longer as the jewel of a brooch or a tiepin for instance, than it would if set in cuff-links or a ring.

Modern lapidary methods make use of power tools and abrasives such as silicon carbide grinding wheels. But when dealing with softer materials, such as aragonite or opal, the learner will do well to start literally from scratch and cut his first cabochons by hand.

Hand kits are relatively inexpensive and consist of a combination coarse and fine grinding stone, a sanding block, felt pads and a polisher. The future gem is either sawn or bought sawn as close as possible to the desired shape. It is then cut by rubbing it against first the coarse and later the fine surfaces of the abrasive.

This is grinding, the process by which the stone is domed to the smooth cabochon shape. The stone is held between the thumb and forefinger, the muscles of the lapidary providing the necessary motion. Even with a stone such as aragonite, progress may not be rapid and patience is needed. But this slow pace is the learner's protection against drastic mistakes.

Sanding is carried out in a similar way. The object here is not to remove material but to smooth away the deep scratches caused by grinding and create a surface capable of being properly polished. Polishing is carried out on the felt pads with pastes made of the polishing agent—it might be pumice, tin oxide or cerium oxide—mixed with water. Pumice might be used first, followed by tin oxide, but each must have a special pad on which no other polish is used.

Between each stage—grinding, sanding, prepolishing and final polishing —both the stone and the hands must be carefully washed to avoid contamination by carrying forward coarse grits. The slower pace of hand work provides invaluable experience for using power tools later but the learner is well advised not to blunt the edge of his enthusiasm by trying to cut and polish tougher stones such as agate by hand.

Another guide to the gemworker, almost as useful in its way as Mohs' scale, is the specific gravity of gemstones. This is given as a figure expressing the ratio of the mass of the stone to that of an equal volume of water. This figure is also an accurate indication of the density of the stone, although specific gravity and density are different things. Density, as showing the compactness and weight of the stone, is of obvious importance to the gemworker.

A wide range of gem materials—I counted more than 50 different items in a recent dealer's catalogue—is available in Australia for the making of cabochons. Most of these stones can be bought in at least two grades, either as slabs from which cabochons may be cut or in a cheaper quality used for tumbling.

Of course, some hobby gemworkers go out and collect their own raw materials from deposits scattered over the face of Australia. An account of this aspect of the hobby was given in my book *Collecting Australian Gemstones*, published in 1965. Despite the fascination of gem fossicking, however, must of the people cutting and polishing gemstones at home either buy from dealers or obtain supplies by swaps with friends living closer to the gemfields.

Although Australia is fortunate in possessing deposits of most of the world's gem materials, it happens in some instances that the stone exists in better quality and larger quantity overseas. Considerable amounts of this high grade material are now imported, particularly from countries of Asia, Africa and both North and South America.

Before we examine in detail the range of gem materials now being cut into cabochons or tumbled into baroques, there is one item of equipment essential to everyone working with gemstones—a jeweller's loupe or eyepiece lens. This need not be an expensive tool but it is essential if we are to study stones closely. Close study is necessary to spot the tiny cracks and flaws in a stone that indicate hidden weaknesses. Such flaws can waste hours of work if they are overlooked and the stone breaks while being cut.

As we have already noted, individual gemstones vary greatly in hardness and texture. These variations extend to other properties. Some stones are less stable than others. Some split readily along certain lines of their natural crystal shape, known as cleavage planes. Some are brittle. Some cannot stand heat.

A variety of techniques have been devised to meet these difficulties,

For example, heat is kept down by the unstinted application of moisture during grinding, sanding and polishing. Dopping—the mounting of a stone on a dopstick with hot sealing-wax—may be carried out with the minimum of heat by using shellac or stones can be cold dopped with a mixture of acetone cement and stiff flour paste.

Various hints of this sort for the treatment of stubborn or difficult stones are included in this list:

## AGATE

Agate is the favourite stone of many hobby gemworkers. Its texture and toughness make for easy working. High-grade material is fairly plentiful and relatively cheap. It takes a high gloss polish with an endless variety of patterns and colours. Of all the baroques and cabochons produced, no two are precisely alike.

The best agates are formed in the steam holes of volcanic rocks. The stone is made of a substance called silica gel, a jellylike mixture of silica and water, which has seeped through the rocks into the cavity. There, over long periods of time, the gel dries and hardens into chalcedonic quartz, coloured by various impurities in the mixture. Agate resists exposure to rain, frost and the atmosphere better than the host rock from which it is eventually freed by weathering.

*Three faces of agate, a master of disguises among gemstones. Left, banded; centre, scenic; right, dendritic.*

The varying conditions in which it is formed explain the vast range of hues and markings of agate. In many cases the silica gel clung to the walls of the cavity, producing a succession of bands, each tracing the outline of the cavity and combining in a web of colour.

The thickness of these bands varies according to the rate at which the silica gel was deposited. The bands often decrease in size gradually to the centre of the cavity, which is often completely filled. It can happen, however, that the centre of the agate is hollow and lined with small quartz crystals.

The lapidary cutting cabochons uses agate in sawn slices or slabs about one-quarter inch in thickness. Much artistry is shown in the selection of an area showing the most beauty and originality of pattern as the future stone. Before the final choice is made, the surface of the slab should be moistened with water and carefully examined under a lens to ensure that no soft pitted spots are within the area intended for cutting and polishing.

Every colour of the rainbow may be seen in banded agate, but these colours are mainly in pastel shades. Vivid colouring often indicates that the agate has been artificially dyed. Banding is the classic agate pattern, but banded agate is only one of many descriptive names given to this beautiful stone.

Eye agate shows a typical concentric marking. Cobra agate is mottled in various colours. In fortification or ruin agate the bands take angular shapes instead of winding in curves. Iris agate shows some iridescence.

Some agates are clouded by pearly translucent material with treelike markings known as dendrites from various impurities. Most familiar of these moss agates are the lacy patterns of blue or black made by manganese oxide, but dendrites can also be red and green. Moss agates used to be called Mocha stones and are known as flower, plume and tree agates, as well as scenic or landscape agates.

A beautiful variety of lace agate, with blue dendrites on a white or faintly coloured base, is found near Norseman, W.A., and in other places. Iron oxide shows as red or brown while green fibres of the mineral chlorite make seaweed agate. Sagenitic agates contain needlelike crystals of other minerals. As might be expected, zebra agate is striped black and white. Onyx has parallel layers of black and white, while sardonyx is red and white and chalcedonyx is grey and white. All forms of onyx used to be especially popular for carving cameos.

Fine agate comes from Brazil and Uruguay, but it is no better than the best of the Queensland stone. The famous centre of Agate Creek, via Forsayth, has been much exploited in recent years, but deposits of high-grade material exist in many parts of Australia. Much colourful imported stone is from India. Lake Superior, Montana and Oregon are famous in the United States.

Agate is hardness 7 on Mohs' scale. Specific gravity varies from 2.5 to 2.8.

## AMAZONITE

Green to blue variety of microcline feldspar which, oddly enough, does not come from Brazil. Three stages of wet sanding—400, 500 and 600 grit—are not too much for this lustrous stone, which polishes well with cerium oxide on a leather lap. Imported material comes from Madagascar, but the best quality amazonite is found at Pikes Peak, Colorado, and in Virginia. Amazonite, or amazonstone, to give its alternative name, is hardness 6-6½ on Mohs' scale. S.G. 2.54 to 2.69.

## ARAGONITE

Aragonite is identical with calcite except in its crystal shape and the fact that it is a little more compact in texture. When pure, it is translucent and white but cabochons are usually cut from banded material, the best of which is found in Mexico. The mineral takes its name from Aragon, Spain, where fine crystals are found. It is so soft that handworking is a safer method than power tools for the inexperienced. It can be polished with cerium oxide on a wax lap. Aragonite varies in hardness from 3½ to 4 on Mohs' scale. S.G. 2.94.

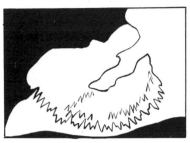

*Aragonite crystals.*

## AZURITE

Another soft stone that is difficult to polish yet highly rewarding to those willing to make the effort. Azurite is another stone that the beginner may prefer to grind by hand. Long and careful wet sanding with a 600 grit cloth is the basis of a successful finish. High polish is best obtained with a paste of cerium oxide on a leather lap. Colours vary from rich Prussian blue to azure although some crystals appear nearly black. Beautiful mineral specimens result from the association of azurite with bright green malachite and many of these were taken in the early days from the Burra Burra mines in South Australia.

Well-known overseas sources are in France, Arizona and Siberia, although a good deal of Australian material comes from Queensland. Azurite is hardness 3½-4 on Mohs' scale. S.G. 3.8.

## BOWENITE

Light yellowish-green gem variety of the rock serpentine, well-known sources of which are the Indian, Chinese and New Zealand deposits. A good deal of Australian material is also available. Hardness 3-4 on Mohs' scale. S.G. 2.5 to 2.7.

## CALCITE

Handworking is the best approach to this difficult material, which is only hardness 3 on Mohs' scale, is heat-shy and splits at the drop of a crystal into tiny rhombohedrons. More than 300 different natural forms of calcite crystals are known. It varies from transparent to opaque and in colour from waterwhite to violet, blue, green, yellow, red, brown and black.

Calcite is one of the fascinating group of minerals which fluoresce under the ultra-violet lamp, varieties containing a trace of manganese being suffused with a peach-pink glow. Some specimens may have to be heated, however, before this effect is obtained.

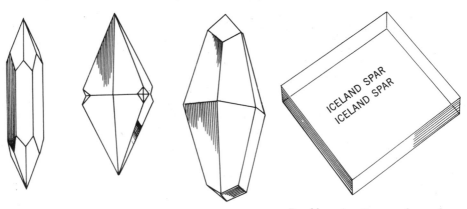

*Some of the 300 different shapes of calcite crystals.*

*Double refraction as shown by a transparent block of the variety of calcite known as Iceland spar.*

Transparent waterwhite crystals known as Iceland spar make fascinating cabochons because of their powerful double refraction (the refractive indices vary from 1.48 to 1.65). Mexican onyx and the yellow travertine calcite also offer interesting possibilities. Polish with cerium oxide by hand or carefully on a wax lap.

Suitable grades of calcite are found all over Australia and world sources of choice crystals are Saxony in West Germany, Cumberland in England and Guanajuato, Mexico. S.G. 2.71.

## CHALCEDONY

Cryptocrystalline—a microscope is needed to show the crystals—variety of quartz, white, blue or grey in colour but most often appearing like watered milk, translucent and showing veins and other markings. Top quality white chalcedony is available from Australian sources, but most blue chalcedony is imported.

Other varieties are carnelian, sard, bloodstone and plasma. Carnelian varies from orange-red to ruby and from opaque to brilliantly transparent in top-grade stones. Brownish-red to yellow-brown stones are called sards. Carnelian takes a high gloss and makes handsome cabochons. In the past it was widely used for seals because wax did not stick to it. Both African and Indian carnelian is imported to Australia.

*Banded carnelian.*

*Australian lucky cross stone—chiastolite, the cross is only seen when the crystals are cut open.*

Bloodstone (also called heliotrope) is a dark green stone flecked with red spots of jasper. A legend claimed that this stone changed water into blood when exposed to sunshine. The same stone with yellow instead of red spots is known as plasma. Again India and South-West Africa are the main sources of this stone. Chalcedony is 6½-7 on Mohs' scale. S.G. 2.5 to 2.8.

## CHERT

Another cryptocrystalline variety of quartz similar to flint but usually in lighter greys and browns or banded. Material varies considerably in quality but is generally available in tumbling grades. Hardness 6½-7 on Mohs' scale. S.G. 2.5 to 2.8.

## CHIASTOLITE

In Spain they say that the cross appeared in crystals of chiastolite when the apostle St. James put his hand on the rock at the place where he was martyred. The name of this variety of the gemstone andalusite comes from the Greek word chiastos meaning crossed, which refers to markings caused by organic impurities which appear as a cross when the brown, grey or bluish crystals are seen in section.

After boundary rider Jim Howden had sent specimens of chiastolite he found on Bimbowrie Station, South Australia, to Queen Victoria in 1897, there was a vogue for a time in "Australian Lucky Cross Stone" cut and polished as charms.

Although it also occurs at places in Western Australia and the Northern Territory, one of the most important sources of chiastolite in the world is Mount Aleone, Bimbowrie, 23 miles north-west of Olary in South Australia.

Andalusite is included among the gem riches of the Minas Gerais province of Brazil and it also occurs in parts of the United States and Europe. Chiastolite found in eastern Finland shows a Maltese cross and is known as maltesite.

Not all chiastolite shows a well-marked cross and some crystals are inclined to split easily, but suitable cross-sections may be sawn for shaping as cabochons if handled carefully. A good finish can be obtained with Linde A on leather. Hardness 7-7½ on Mohs' scale, but this may vary. S.G. 3.22 to 3.29.

## CHRYSOPRASE

Bright apple green variety of chalcedony, coloured by nickel oxide. Flaws and cracks are common and the stone is often streaked with white. Use plenty of water when grinding and sanding for heat will bleach the colour from chrysoprase. Polish with putty powder mixed to a cream on a leather buff. Deposits near Marlborough, Queensland, are producing some of the finest gem quality stones, while other sources are Oregon and California in the United States, Silesia in Europe and Comet Vale, Western Australia.

A duller darker green variety of chalcedony is called prase. Both this stone and chrysoprase are hardness 6½-7 on Mohs' scale. S.G. 2.5 to 2.8.

## GARNET

Grossularite garnet from South Africa is available for Australian hobby gemworkers in a variety of colours—hyacinth red, apricot-shaded cinnamon stone, and the green variety incorrectly known as Transvaal jade. Green grossularite is often mottled with white or discoloured and is then regarded as tumbling grade material.

Dark-red almandite garnet, known as carbuncle, sometimes showing a moving four-pointed star of light as a result of inclusions in the crystal, is also cut as a cabochon. These stones are rather brittle and care should be taken in both grinding and sanding. At least three stages of wet sanding are followed by cerium oxide on felt for the best results. Garnets are hardness 6-7½ on Mohs' scale. S.G. Grossularite, 3.5 to 3.7, almandite, 3.7 to 4.2.

## GOLDSTONE

Artificial gem material made of glass of various colours—blue, green, brown, etc.—with glittering metal fragments included. Material imported from Italy is supplied in both cabochon and tumbling grades. Prepolishing with pumice powder followed by cerium oxide on a felt buff is the recipe for an attractive polish on goldstone. Hardness 5-6 on Mohs' scale. S.G. 2.21.

## IOLITE

This is gem quality of the mineral cordierite, which is also known by the erroneous but colourful name of water sapphire. It varies in quality from translucent to transparent and occurs commonly in the various shades of blue from which the popular name is derived.

Many crystals possess the peculiar property of showing three colours —blue, brown and yellow—and a cube can be cut with different coloured sides if the rough crystal is properly oriented. This means that to obtain a good stone for jewellery purposes, one must take care to cut it so that the best colour—a clear blue—is showing.

Iolite is often faceted as well as being cut as cabochons. Linde A on a leather lap gives the best polish. Most imported material in Australia comes from India and Ceylon and good iolite is also found in several parts of the United States. Hardness 7-7½ on Mohs' scale. S.G. 2.6.

## JADE

Nephrite, with jadeite, one of the twin minerals known as jade, is imported from New Zealand where it was once used for weapons and ornaments by the Maoris, who managed to carve it without the aid of metal tools. Pure nephrite is white and it also can be brown, mauve, blue, yellow, red, grey and black as well as the well-known green.

Diligent wet sanding with the 400, 500 and 600 cloths, followed by polishing with a well-watered mixture of Linde A powder or chromium oxide on a leather buff, is the way to get a high polish on jade. New sources of nephrite have recently been discovered in the United States, while the ancient deposits of Chinese jade are in Central Asia. Apple-green jadeite is mined in Upper Burma, Guatemala and California. Both minerals are hardness 6½-7 on Mohs' scale. S.G. Jadeite, 3.3 to 3.5, nephrite 2.9 to 3.1.

## JASPER

This opaque cryptocrystalline variety of quartz occurs in almost all the colours of the spectrum—red, yellow, brown, grey, green, blue. Striped or ribbon jasper is banded in various contrasting colours. Various names have been coined for patterned stones such as aboriginal jasper, leopard jasper and orbicular jasper, while a jasper bearing flower-like patterns is known as poppy stone.

*Banded jasper is beautiful, but this gem can also be a fascinating picture stone, as on the right.*

Jasper takes a high polish but gemworkers should look out for the soft, pitted spots common on slabs. These spots are impossible to polish but they may be easily seen and avoided by wetting the surface of the slab. Some fine stones have been cut from Western Australian jaspilite, a rock consisting of bands of red jasper alternating with black hematite. Jasper is hardness 6½-7 on Mohs' scale. S.G. 2.5 to 2.8.

## LABRADORITE

One of the plagioclase feldspars, this stone is basically grey in colour but good specimens show a play of colours, usually blue or green but sometimes yellow or red. The best material, found on the Labrador coast, is imported from Canada, but the stone occurs in various parts of the United States and Europe. Labradorite is hardness 6 on Mohs' scale. S.G. 2.69.

## LAPIS LAZULI

This azure blue rock, sometimes glittering with specks of metallic pyrite, was the sapphire of olden times. Gem quality lapis lazuli has been mined in Afghanistan from the dawn of history. Other sources of top quality material are in Siberia, Chile and Colorado. Sodalite is one of the three main ingredients of lapis, which is hardness 6 on Mohs' scale. S.G. 2.45 to 2.90.

## MALACHITE

Bright green copper carbonate, more common than azurite. Its crystal form is rare, malachite usually occurring in rounded masses banded in light and dark green from which beautiful cabochons may be cut.

*Malachite.*

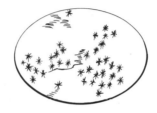

*Opalite.*

Some of the finest crystal specimens have come from Mount Isa, Queensland, and Cobar, N.S.W., while the Burra Burra mines of South Australia were a famous source of the massive stone. Now only scattered fragments remain to be picked from the spoil heaps of the old mine. Most of the malachite on sale in Australia now is from African sources, Katanga in the Congo, Rhodesia and South West Africa. Widespread deposits also occur in the Western United States and there are famous mines in the Ural Mountains of Russia. Malachite is hardness $3\frac{1}{2}$-4 on Mohs' scale. S.G. 4. Cutting and polishing techniques are similar to azurite.

## MOONSTONE

Translucent specimens of three different varieties of feldspar—orthoclase, albite and oligoclase—are all cut and polished as moonstones. All show a delicate pearly opalescence caused by the reflection of light from thin layers of material making up the stone. Most moonstones are pale milky white and examples of the variety adularia with bluish sheen are the most prized. All varieties are of hardness 6-$6\frac{1}{2}$ on Mohs' scale. S.G. 2.5 to 2.6.

Pink moonstone is the less common mineral scapolite, which has a hardness of $5\frac{1}{2}$-6. Fine yellow crystals of scapolite found in Madagascar are also cut as gems.

## PYRITE

This common brassy yellow mineral, iron pyrites or iron disulphide to give its scientific name, is also called "fool's gold" because of the fossickers it has tricked in the past and continues to trick. To complete the tally of aliases, it is also known as marcasite to the jewellery trade, especially when faceted as little rose-cut gems.

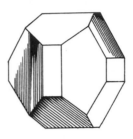

*Two of the 60 types of pyrite crystals.*

Mineralogists divide marcasite from pyrite according to the natural crystal systems. Hardness 6 to 6½ on Mohs' scale, pyrite cuts to a nice cabochon if you can bear the stink of sulphur and the messy green-black residue, but is difficult to polish. Try tin oxide on leather and finish off with the paste only just damp. It can be faceted, too. Gem quality pyrite is found at a number of places in Australia, but the celebrated world source is Rio Tinto, Spain. S.G. 4.95 to 5.10.

## OBSIDIAN

Volcanic glass, usually black or black-green but sometimes brown, red, grey or banded with two or more of these colours. Snowflake obsidian, one of the most attractive United States varieties, is shiny black with white inclusions of christobalite and is a stone that looks well set in silver.

*Two sorts of lovely obsidian, left, snowflake, right, flowering.*

Other attractive obsidians show golden and silvery sheen while rainbow obsidian gleams with many hues. Rounded pieces of obsidian from the Western United States are known as Apache tears. All varieties are hardness 5-5½ on Mohs' scale. S.G. 2.3 to 2.6. Prepolishing with pumice powder after careful wet sanding is the method producing the best polish. Low-grade obsidian merges into pitchstone or rhyolite.

## OPAL

Broadly speaking, there are two sorts of opal—precious, which shows a play of colours, and common, which does not. The colours are fiery reds and yellows, greens and blues which shimmer and sparkle as the stone is turned in the light. They are caused by reflections from layers of micro-crystalline silica of which the opal is composed.

Some opal shows fluorescence, glowing white or yellow when exposed to ultra-violet light. The celebrated opal buyer Tullie Wollaston wore a stone known as The Star of Bethlehem as a tiepin. In his book *They Struck Opal*, Wollaston's associate Ted Murphy writes: "It could be seen shining on the darkest night before its wearer became visible. In a bank vault I could see it glowing like a red star, and its perpetual brilliance never faded."

Precious opal is of two sorts—black and white. These descriptions refer to the body colour of the stone, one showing its colours against a dark or blue background and the other against a background of milky white. Of the two, black opal is the most colourful and therefore most prized. The mines at Lightning Ridge, N.S.W., produced the finest black opal in the world.

Pattern and colour decide value. Patterns include pinfire, which shows its colour as sparks of light; flash, vivid, broad and irregular rolling colours; and harlequin, in which the colour is in an orderly pattern of squares. Red fire or reds combined with greens and blues are favourite colours.

Before cutting an opal cabochon thoroughly examine the stone with a glass in a good light. Look for the fire and for the flaws. Avoid the last-named and centre your stone on the area of most fire.

Often common opal or potch has to be cut away. If so, use water in the coolant tank of your saw, because opal soaks up kerosene, which dulls and discolours it. Grind carefully with a gentle pressure and keep down friction by continually moving the stone on the wheel. Heat from any source can cause opal to crack and craze disastrously, so be cautious with the spirit lamp when dopping. Shellac is a useful dopping medium because of its low melting point.

Opal is hardness 5-6½ on Mohs' scale and like other soft stones, is all the better for three stages of wet sanding. Tin oxide on a muslin buff will produce an excellent polish although jeweller's rouge is the classic for opal.

Wafer thin slices of opal have to be strengthened by being made into doublets, which means cementing the opal to a piece of black potch with a mixture of melted shellac and lampblack or black Araldite.

By far the largest share of Australia's opal comes from the two South Australian fields of Andamooka and Coober Pedy, although recent finds have increased output from White Cliffs, N.S.W. Small quantities of fine black opal continue to come from Lightning Ridge. S.G. 2.0 to 2.2. Matrix opal—rock containing opal—is also cut and polished when suitable.

## OPALITE

Dendrites, the branching patterns formed by manganese oxide or iron oxide, make common opal into a charming and distinctive Australian gemstone. Sometimes the result is hard to tell from moss agate.

Common opal is often a rather drab yellowish-green, but it also occurs in more attractive shades of pink, milky-white and pale blue. When marked with black or red-brown dendrites these stones are known as lace or moss opalites.

Material from Queensland and Western Australia is sold in both tumbling and cabochon grades and has become a very popular gemstone among hobby workers. S.G. 1.85 to 2.2.

## PETALITE

A white variety of one of the lithium minerals, mainly used for tumbling. Hardness 7 on Mohs' scale.

## PETRIFIED WOOD

Fossilised timber in which the organic structure has been replaced by one or more of a number of mineral substances. The most common of these substances is chalcedony, which means that most petrified wood is in fact silicified wood. In other cases opal replaces the vegetable matter of the tree, resulting in opalised wood, which is a softer material.

Petrified wood comes in every shade of grey and brown ranging to red and orange, patterned and veined in a variety of colours. Some petrified wood shows a similarity in colours and markings to agate and is known as agatized wood. Commonly, the process of petrifaction is so perfect that the grain of the original timber can be seen clearly.

Petrified wood varies in colour and texture according to locality and also according to the species of the original tree. Petrified palm, for instance, shows characteristic patterns and warm colouring. Much Australian wood is, of course, petrified eucalypt. An illustration of how this material can vary is seen at Wollongong, N.S.W., where the wood occurs in soft shades of brown and dark grey, while at Bellambi, less than six miles away, the colours are quite different, appearing in lively reds, tans and yellow-browns. However these stones are mainly chips from aborigines' tools and may have been brought from a distance.

The quality of petrified wood varies naturally according to the extent of silicification. The best material cuts almost as well as agate and takes a resplendent polish. Like agate, it at once delights and challenges the lapidary to select exactly the right area for his cabochon from the slab. Cerium oxide on leather is recommended for polishing.

Inexpensive and easy to collect, being found in all parts of Australia, petrified wood also makes some of the most attractive tumbled stones. It varies in hardness on Mohs' scale from the $5\frac{1}{2}$ of opalised wood to the 7 of silicified wood.

## PREHNITE

A pale green to yellowish brown, transparent to translucent stone, the cloudy markings and colour graduations of which make interesting and attractive cabochons. It may also be faceted. Linde A on a leather lap is recommended for polishing.

Prehnite occurs in New South Wales, Queensland and Western Australia and is particularly a Sydney gemstone, owing to the deposits at Prospect. The stone was originally discovered in South Africa. Hardness on Mohs' scale is $6-6\frac{1}{2}$. S.G. 2.9.

## PSILOMELANE

Handsome gem quality of the common manganese ore, black or dark grey in colour, sometimes banded. The name is unusual. It is formed from two Greek words meaning smooth and black. It is harder than most of the manganese oxides. It occurs in Australia and overseas.

## QUARTZ

Many crystalline varieties of quartz make beautiful gems, mostly as cabochons although many may also be cut as faceted stones. One of these quartz gems, the amethyst, was once held in far greater esteem. But fashion changed although the attractive purple and violet stones are now favourites with hobby gemworkers. Amethysts should be handled tenderly, because they have a tendency to crack, especially when overheated.

*Black manganese oxide markings on the pink gemstone often make rhodonite an attractive picture stone. Mr B. D. Hoggins, of Hobart, Tasmania, sees a village church spire through trees in this specimen he collected.*

*Petrified wood often shows the grain markings of the original timber.*

These weaknesses are shared by rose quartz, a rose-red or pink variety, yellow quartz, the top quality of which is called citrine, and smoky quartz or cairngorm, which varies from tawny to almost black in colour. The common white crystals are known as milky quartz. All these stones as well as the lesser-known blue quartz, hold rewards for the enthusiast prepared to take extra trouble to cut them as cabochons.

Among the most delightful quartz stones are crystals containing other mineral impurities. Most popular of these is aventurine, a stone of various colours flecked with glittering scales of mica or hematite. Fibres of asbestos enclosed in the crystal make quartz cat's eye, a stone showing a gleaming band of light. Grass-stone is transparent quartz containing long fine interlacing light-brown crystals of rutile. For this stone and others which include crystals of tourmaline, actinolite and goethite, such romantic names as Venus-hair stone, Cupid's darts and Arrows of Love have been coined.

Fine crystals of many varieties of quartz are found at various places in Australia, particularly the New England district of New South Wales, and Gladstone, Tasmania. Most imported material is from Brazil or India. Quartz is hardness 7 on Mohs' scale. S.G. 2.6 to 2.7.

## RIBBONSTONE

Silicified banded shale from various localities in north-western Queensland, showing a variety of patterns and colours. Mohs' scale hardness is 6½-7.

## RHODONITE

Rose-red, pink or brownish ore of manganese, usually veined attractively with black manganese oxide. Careful high-speed sanding with plenty of water, followed by a well-watered Linde A polishing mixture on a leather lap is the right way to treat rhodonite, which is hardness 5-6 on Mohs' scale. Rhodochrosite, the pink or rose-red carbonate of manganese, is even softer, being hardness $3\frac{1}{2}$-$4\frac{1}{2}$. S.G. 3.5 to 3.6.

Top quality rhodonite and rhodochrosite are mined at various places in Australia, including Broken Hill, N.S.W., a celebrated source of gem quality material.

## SODALITE

The popular gem variety of this silicate mineral is an opaque azure blue, although specimens can be white, grey, red, yellow or green. A rather soft stone—hardness $5\frac{1}{2}$-6 on Mohs' scale—it requires careful wet sanding followed by cerium oxide on a leather buff. Some nice sodalite comes from Queensland but material imported from Canada is of rich colours that make a cabochon to be remembered. S.G. 2.2 to 2.3.

## SUNSTONE

This aventurine feldspar shows a wonderful golden sheen reflected from multitudes of tiny crystals of nematite or goethite. Material available in Australia is imported from India more often than not, but the finest sunstone is mined in Norway. This is a reddish variety oligoclase feldspar, while a green microcline sunstone is found in Pennsylvania, U.S.A. Hardness 6-$6\frac{1}{2}$ on Mohs' scale. S.G. 2.5 to 2.6.

## TIGER'S-EYE

This stone, said to be the most popular with Australian gemworkers, is what the mineralogist calls a pseudomorph. Both tiger's-eye and the related stone hawk's-eye are composed of silica that has taken over the structure of the asbestos mineral crocidolite. Loosely speaking, one might call both petrified asbestos. The only difference between the two is their colour. In the case of tiger's-eye, iron in the mineral has oxidised to red or golden-yellow. In hawk's-eye, however, the crocidolite is still blue.

Fibres should be parallel to the base of the cut stone and tin oxide on leather is hard to beat for the final polish. Grinding and sanding must be carried out at right angles to the grain.

Crocidolite deposits in Western Australia provide top-grade material but the most famous world source is in Griqualand, South Africa.

## TURQUOISE

This stone should never be sawn with a lapidary saw that has kerosene as the coolant or it is likely to turn a hideous shade of green. Turquoise is porous and should be kept out of oil, soapsuds or any dirty water. Only a minority of stones occurring naturally show the desired shade of pale blue. Most show traces of grey or green.

A light hand in grinding and sanding is essential to success with turquoise, which is only hardness 6. A creamy mixture of tin oxide on a padded leather buff soon produces a high polish. At no stage should the stone be allowed to get hot or it may start to show white spots.

For more than a thousand years turquoise has been mined at Nishapur, in Persia, while mines on the Sinai Peninsula of Egypt are even more ancient. Now the finest quality stones are found in Mexico and the south-west United States, where they are still prized by the American Indians, especially the Navajos.

Turquoise is found in places along the eastern seaboard of Australia, in Queensland, New South Wales, Victoria and Tasmania, as well as Mount Painter and Kadina South in South Australia, but it is mostly green. Some fine blue stone occurs in thin veins near Mansfield, Vic. S.G. 2.6 to 2.8. Rock flecked and coloured with turquoise is sometimes cut and polished as turquoise matrix.

Other materials, such as the decorative rock trachyte, are sometimes cut as cabochons by amateurs, most of whom are always willing to experiment.

All stones showing interior rays of light in the form of cat's-eyes or stars are cut in the cabochon style to obtain the best effect.

These stones include the variety of chrysoberyl known as cat's-eye or cymophane, which is greenish in colour with a silky lustre, as well as occasional aquamarines and zircons, and those magnificent rubies and sapphires which display a six-pointed star when cut as cabochons.

The light rays shown in all these gems—phenomena technically described as chatoyancy and asterism—are due to inclusions of foreign matter in the stone, often hair-like crystals of rutile. A stone of this sort which is cut at right angles to the vertical axis of the gem crystal will show a star while one cut parallel to the axis shows a cat's-eye.

Because of their hardness—9 on Mohs' scale—sapphires have to be cut and polished as cabochons on faceting equipment—flat metal laps charged with diamond dust.

Unfortunately, however, the opportunity to tackle stones of this merit rarely occurs for the hobby gemworker.

The smaller tumbling machine which turns a barrel of about half-a-gallon capacity is best suited to the needs of the hobby gemworker. Illustrating this type of machine is Australian Lapidary Supplies Model M11-1. Below: The Australian-made Galaxy tumbling barrel. It is specially shaped to oscillate, weave and keep the contents constantly moving in every direction.

The popular Mighty Mite tilted tumbling
machine is now also available as the Multi-
Mite, which rotates three one-quart plastic jars.
In these jars small quantities of stones of
different hardness can be processed at the same
time.

# FINDINGS AND SETTINGS

The range of bought settings for tumbled stones in sterling silver and gold plate as well as base metal alloys has been extended to include almost every imaginable jewellery item.

*Devices for setting baroques — above, spring bracelet; right, cufflinks; below, two ring styles. The rings also have adjustable shanks.*

*Two tricky little brooch settings designed to effectively show off tumbled gemstones.*

*Contrast in bracelet styles: left, an ideal gift for a small girl; above, more sophisticated designs. Each displays lustrous tumbled gemstones in all the colourings of the rainbow.*

*Novelty designs — tumbled gems make the paints on an artists palette brooch; opal chips in a clear plastic globe form an unusual earring, while a cage of silver or gold wire can form the basis of bracelets or pendants.*

# COMBINATION UNITS

*Workroom space is often the hobby gemworker's greatest problem and combination lapidary machines make the best use of it. For instance, this Robilt 6in. saw / grinder / sander / polisher takes up only 15in. by 18in. by 9in. and is no more than 30lb. in weight.*

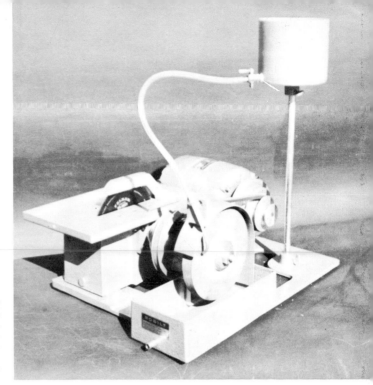

*Below: This combined grinder / sander / polisher from Thompson's Lapidary Supplies includes three sanding discs. The firm specialises in kits which hobbyists can assemble themselves.*

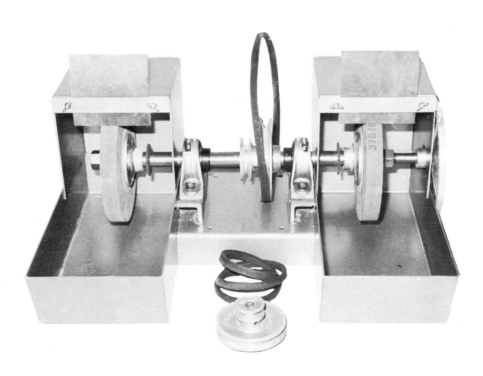

*This 8in. diamond blade trim saw made by R. L. & W. P. Hall of Cairns, Qld., can also slab any size gemstone that the 4in. by 2in. clamp will hold.*

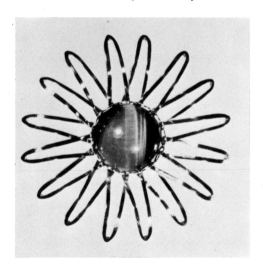

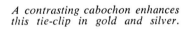

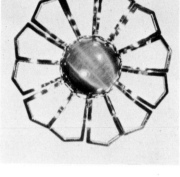

*Charming open settings such as these suit chatoyant tiger's-eye, aventurine or opal.*

*A contrasting cabochon enhances this tie-clip in gold and silver.*

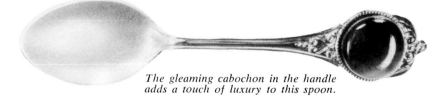

*The gleaming cabochon in the handle adds a touch of luxury to this spoon.*

# CABOCHON SETTINGS

*These brooch settings are exquisite in either gold or silver combined with perfectly shaped and polished cabochons in bold colours. Alternatively, small tumbled stones can be set in the spray and leaf on the right.*

*His and her birthday stones side-by-side in this ring.*

Settings shown on this and other pages are by courtesy of Mr. Elio Re, of Australian Lapidary Supplies.

*Two classic bracelet designs for cabochons which are cut as triangles in the one on the right.*

*Jewellery such as these examples from the collection of Mrs. Elizabeth Fry of the Lapidary Club of Victoria illustrates the beauty and variety of objects which can be made with bought settings.*

## COSTS

At the end of 1966 Australian lapidary supply houses were offering gemstones for tumbling and cabochons at the following prices: Queensland agate, $5 to 30 cents a lb.; imported agate, $1.25; amazonite, $3.40; amethyst, $6 to $1.95; aventurine, $1.40; blue aventurine, $4.40 to $2.40; Western Australian bloodstone, 75 cents; imported bloodstone, $4.40 to $1.40; chert, $1 to 60 cents; chrysoprase, $6 to 60 cents an oz.; garnet, $1.42 an oz. to $10 a lb.; goldstone, $3.25 to $2.50 a lb.; jasper, $4.40 to 60 cents; chiastolite crystals, 10 cents each; iolite, $10.25 a lb. to $1.69 an oz.; labradorite, $5.95 a lb.; lapis lazuli, $3.6 a lb. to $4.25 an oz.; malachite, $10 a lb. to 42 cents an oz.; moonstone, $1.50 to 40 cents an oz.; snowflake obsidian, $1.25 a lb.; slabbed flowering obsidian, 35 cents sq. in.; opal, $60 to $ an oz.; black opal, $75 a carat to $5 an oz.; opal matrix, $3 to $8 an oz.; opalite, 75 cents to 60 cents a lb.; opalised wood, $1.25 a lb.; petrified wood, 60 cents to 10 cents a lb.; petalite, 50 cents to 30 cents a lb.; prase, $1.50 to 30 cents; prehnite, $2; quartz, $10 to 20 cents; rutilated quartz, $2.80; Queensland ribbonstone, $1.75 to 80 cents; rhodochrosite, $3.70; rhodonite, 90 cents to 40 cents; sodalite, $1.75; sunstone, $1.12 an oz.; tiger's-eye, $2.80 to $1.20 a lb.; turquoise, $6.76 an oz.

A suitable jeweller's lens should cost about 60 cents and a complete hand kit $5.50.

These prices are, of course, subject to fluctuation and cannot be regarded as binding on any lapidary supply house. Prices of most gemstones vary a great deal according to quality and this can only be judged accurately by examining the material.

# 2

# CHEAP AND ATTRACTIVE

SIT AWHILE ON A PEBBLY BEACH and listen to the world's oldest lapidary machine at work. Every splash and surge of the tide is followed by a loud clatter as the sea picks up the pebbles and dashes them one against the other.

Over restless centuries these pebbles have worn smooth and round. See how they gleam under the water, bright as jewels. But these jewels are only make-believe for they turn dull and drab as soon as the beach is dry.

Hobby gemworkers nowadays have machines that not only imitate the action of the sea but improve on it. In a few weeks these tumbling machines grind gemstones into smooth rounded shapes that it would take many years to produce naturally—and, unlike the beach pebbles, these stones have a polish that is enduring as well as brilliant.

The sea tumbles the pebbles on the beach with the ebb and flow of the tide. But the tide of the tumbling machine rises and falls not four times in 24 hours but anything from 15 to 40 times a minute according to the speed at which the machine is turning.

The power that provides this constant motion is usually that of an electric motor, varying from $\frac{1}{4}$ to $\frac{3}{4}$ h.p. or more. This is connected by various devices, either pulleys or gears, so that it spins one or more tumbling barrels.

In the type of machine most often made by home handymen, the barrels are turned by a pair of rubber-covered steel rollers mounted parallel to each other about 4 in. apart. The rollers are connected to each other and to the motor by a series of pulleys.

Tumbling machines work almost too well. A machine operating only one barrel with a capacity of one gallon can process about 1,000 gemstones in one batch.

This mass production cannot be avoided. It is an essential part of the tumbling process. The effectiveness of the abrasive mixture used depends to a large extent on the weight and bulk of the contents of the barrel. In the case of the roller-type machine, barrels must be loaded to at least half their capacity for satisfactory operation. This means that even a half-gallon barrel on these machines can hardly process fewer than around 300 stones at each operation.

A popular type of manufactured machine, which operates tilted at an angle between vertical and horizontal, is a little more flexible in its load requirements but every rotary tumbling machine, whatever its design, has a minimum load below which it cannot grind and polish properly.

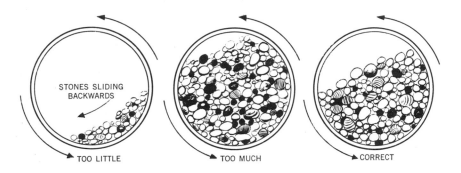

*The tumbling load: If the barrel is underfilled, the stones do not polish. If it is overfilled, tumbling takes far longer because movement of the stones is choked. Between half and three-quarters full is right. All sizes of stones should make up the load for best results.*

This over-production problem is aggravated by the fact that the best results are only obtained when stones tumbled together are of similar hardness and composition. Otherwise, chipping and bruising—the appearance of a white film around the edges of the softer stones—is liable to occur.

The only real answer to this embarrassment of riches is to set rigid standards of quality on tumbled stones. Any stone showing a chip or a flaw or an inferior polish should be discarded. However this is not a solution that will appeal to every enthusiast who has spent time, money and effort to obtain materials and tumble them.

Yet it is only by hobby gemworkers generally setting the highest standards that tumbling can maintain its status as a means of producing cheap and attractive costume jewellery. In recent years far too many inferior tumbled stones have been seen around made up as cheap—and not so cheap—jewellery. If the producers had any thought for maintaining the reputation of tumbled gemstones this material would have been either reprocessed or discarded.

Without a doubt, over-production and inferior quality have already brought tumbling into some disrepute. Yet one has only to see the products of those hobby gemworkers who are specialists and indeed perfectionists in the art to know that this is an injustice. Tumbled stones which have been selected with care and processed with skill are gems in their own right. Tastefully combined with the better quality settings now available from most lapidary dealers, they make up into costume jewellery that has the professional look.

One example that springs to mind is a brooch in which one lady member of the Lapidary Society of New South Wales takes deserved pride. It consists of no more than a tumbled beach pebble of a quartzy appearance and a simple bought setting, apparently cast in some copper-zinc alloy in the shape of a flower about 3 in. long.

The special attraction of the piece is due to a combination of good design in the setting and unique colour in the stone. This is a clear apricot touched with white and brought to such an excellent polish that the stone seems almost translucent. This brooch cost little more than a dollar to make and yet it is a work of art.

The secret of this kind of success in tumbling begins with good fortune and good judgment in the choice of material. Neither of these qualities are matters easily taught, although experience helps in visualising what rough stones will look like when they have been processed. But hard work, patience and skill is needed as well as an element of good luck.

*This bought finding is attractively designed but what lifts this brooch out of the rut is the glossy apricot-coloured beach pebble with white markings cemented in the centre of the flower.*

First steps in tumbling depend on the condition of the rough material. A selection of beach pebbles will already be in rounded natural shapes suitable for loading into the tumbler. But crushed stone will be in angular shapes bearing sharp jagged edges. Some pieces may be too large for tumbling and will have to be broken with a rock pick or hammer, if no better means, such as a diamond saw, is available.

Unless this crushed stone is of a soft nature, that is to say hardness 5 or below, it will take many extra hours of grinding in the tumbler to reduce it to the desired rounded shapes. Even if the stone is soft enough to grind easily, some waste of material and loss of effort is involved.

For the hobby gemworker who aims at perfection in tumbled stones, the first task when dealing with crushed material is preforming. Preforming consists of grinding away the corners and angles of rough stones by hand on a silicon carbide wheel. The coarsest grade of wheel available—usually 100 grit—is the right one.

As with all rough grinding, the wheel must be kept wet all the time when in use and not too much pressure exerted on its surface. Grinding wheels take quite a bashing during preforming anyway and if you have an old wheel handy it is as well to use it. Bear in mind that rough treatment of the grinding wheel can burn out the electric motor, too.

All the rough edges are ground away by applying the stone by hand to the edge of the wheel at about centre level. Exert a steady, even pressure and concentrate on keeping the stone moving across the thickness of the wheel. You may think it worth while only to preform the larger fragments of softer stones, but in the case of harder material—say, when tumbling agate—only the small chips should be left untreated.

Preforming demands both patience and enthusiasm. The treatment of sufficient petrified wood or agate to load a half-gallon barrel may take a couple of days and the temptation to try a short-cut, such as including some fragments of broken grinding wheel in the mixture, is sometimes irresistible.

The use of a worn-out silicon carbide wheel as a tumbling agent can considerably reduce the time spent in grinding rough stones. The wheel must be broken into pieces of about the same size as the material being tumbled. For that matter every tumbling load should contain a variety of sizes to assist in carrying the abrasive to all parts of the mixture.

Grinding wheels consist of silicon carbide grit of various sizes—in the case of the coarse wheel usually 100 grit—bonded with clay and baked like a brick. Pieces of this material make a very harsh abrasive, the use of which should be restricted to such tough stones as agate and other crypto-crystalline varieties of quartz.

Every vestige of broken wheel must be picked out before a finer grade of abrasive is introduced. If it should be overlooked, even the smallest piece would disfigure stones being processed later on.

The use of broken grinding wheel can cut down tumbling by many scores of hours but preforming offers other advantages than that of speeding up the grinding process. As each stone is given individual treatment, any pitted areas or other blemishes can be removed before it goes into the tumbler. Better still, art has a chance to improve on nature in the matter of shapes and markings. Often a lack of balance or proportion can be put right by judicious grinding or some extraneous mark erased from an otherwise perfect pattern.

Each item of preformed material is a gemstone in its own right which has been treated according to its individual merits. That is why the finest quality tumbled stones have invariably been preformed and the real tumbling enthusiast insists on preforming whenever he loads his machine.

Transparent or translucent stones which have included fibres or crystals, such as rutilated quartz, can be clouded with dirt and polishing powders during tumbling. A safeguard against this is provided by soaking the rough stone in a sodium silicate (waterglass) solution. A few drops of detergent help the sodium silicate to penetrate into the stone and seal the surface of it. Soaking the stone in clean warm water for seven or eight days will get rid of the silicate. This method will work with any stone in which minute cracks or fissures occur and is also useful when sawing, grinding and polishing gems generally.

Before anyone can start to tumble gemstones, the obvious essential is a tumbling machine. At one time there was a feeling that a couple of old paint cans kept revolving by a patched-up refrigerator motor constituted a satisfactory machine. Now it is widely recognised that a scientifically-designed appliance does a quicker job more efficiently.

This is not to say that factory-made machines are all perfect. Probably the best designed and most efficient tumblers are numbered among those devised by the many engineers who have made lapidary their hobby. But there is now a range of models on the market sufficient to satisfy the needs of everyone interested in tumbling stones.

The roller-type machine still retains its early popularity. The flexibility of this type of machine is demonstrated by a model produced by Thompson Lapidary Supplies, the Brisbane firm, which can handle either a couple of four-gallon barrels for the commercial producer or three half-gallon containers for the hobbyist.

Perhaps the most versatile machine on the market is a Gemmasta roller-type unit. The tumbling barrels on this machine consist of PVC plastic closed at each end by metal plates secured with wing nuts. As the plastic is available in tubes of 4 in., 5 in. and 6 in. diameter, a great variety of barrel sizes can be made by cutting it into the various lengths. These barrels can be bought ready-made in sizes that can tumble from 6 lb. to 1½ lb. of stones.

The trend is towards the smaller machine adapted to the hobbyist's needs. The Queensland firm of R. L. and W. P. Hall, of Cairns, put out a roller-type tumbler with two one-quart plastic containers. Jack Taylor's Mighty Mite, best-known of the tilted machines, now also appears as the Multi-mite with three one-quart plastic containers. This ingenious device allows small quantities of stones of different hardness which have to be tumbled apart to still be dealt with at one time on the same machine. Of course, this also applies to the horizontal machines designed to take quart cans.

Controversy rages among tumbling enthusiasts on the merits of the two types of machine. The tilted machines have a couple of things to be said in their favour—because of their stance they do not need to be burped or de-gassed and their contents are more easily examined and tended. This second advantage is countered by the fact that the action of the tilted machine is not so positive as that of the horizontal type and unless the operator keeps an eye on it there is a tendency for the abrasive to settle at the base of the container.

Not having to be burped at regular intervals is the biggest advantage of the tilted machine. The build-up of carbide gas in horizontal tumblers during grinding can be sufficient to cause an explosion or at least to cause containers to leak at the seams. Therefore the horizontal machine has to be fitted with a small gas cock or release screw and the operator must remember to burp this at least once every 36 hours.

Another problem for the man building his own tumbling machine is some device for slowing down the operating speed for polishing. Commercial models are usually supplied with either two-speed pulleys or some sort of variable gear device. The easiest way out with the home-made machine is to fit the barrel kept for polishing with specially thick rubber rings which can be bought from most lapidary dealers. These decrease the number of revolutions by increasing the diameter of the barrel in relation to the drive roller.

It is claimed that the tilted machines are less noisy—a factor of some importance to flat-dwellers—but noise depends more on the size and efficiency of the machine than anything else. By far the most noise is created by the contents of the tumbling barrel as it revolves and a lot of noise usually indicates the machine is doing a poor job of tumbling.

Smaller machines are quieter, of course. The increasing use of plastic containers or rubber-lined cans also cuts down noise, but plastic containers do not usually wear as well as metal ones unless they are made of heavy duty material.

The efficiency of a tumbling machine is based on the shape of the container or barrel. This must be designed to create the greatest possible movement in the load as it turns so that abrasive or polishing compounds pervade the barrel and reach the surface of every stone in it.

In the roller-type machines movement within the load increases with the width of the barrel and octagon-shaped barrels produce an even more marked effect. The interior of the new Australian-produced Galaxy tumbling barrel presents a continuously tilted surface as it revolves, keeping the stones in a state of constant motion. Despite this extra agitating action, the Galaxy can be operated more quickly than either the hexagonal or cylindrical barrels and therefore completes processes more quickly.

Experiments have been going on for some time in Australia with the vibratory tumbling machines popular in the United States. I asked Jack Taylor to comment on these machines and this is what he told me: "At the moment I can't see that these vibratory tumblers are going to be very successful because they have to work so quickly that they make a lot of noise and create a lot of vibration. They shake the tables and when you put them on a concrete floor they make even more noise.

"They work well, though. I made a vibrating tumbler and it worked beautifully. I put a quarter horsepower motor on it, but this must have been too big because after a couple of days we shook the base off the motor. We welded the base on again and the next thing it shook all the cans to pieces.

"But it did do the work. You could see the stones trying to burrow down all the time and as they went down, they were pushing others up. The action was really good. They'll tackle the hardest stones and I found they cut our agates very quickly.

"Vibratory tumblers are quicker, too. But I can't see how the amateur can use them at the moment because they would make too much noise in a house. They do work faster, but then, speed is not essential."

By present methods, a complete tumbling operation takes about six weeks if the machine is kept in constant operation. In making up the load it is important to see that the varieties of stones included are of about the same hardness. Ribbonstone, jasper and chalcedony can be tumbled together, for instance, but no varieties of crystalline quartz should be included because of the risk of chipping.

A half-gallon container will require about 4 lb. of stones varying in size from mere chips to more than an inch in diameter. Add 5 oz. of 80 silicon carbide grit and water until it rises more than an inch above the level of the stones and a teaspoonful of household detergent if the stones are very hard.

Secure the lid properly and start up the tumbler. Listen to the sounds coming from the revolving barrel. If they are regular and rhythmic, all is well. But if the sounds are jerky or irregular or indicate that the stones are striking each other too fiercely, check that the speed is not too fast and the load neither too small nor too large—the barrel should be a little under three-quarters full, with the contents covered by water.

Stones in a barrel that is insufficiently loaded usually end up as unpolishable flats while the overloaded barrel grinds well enough but takes a long time over it. Stones in a barrel spinning too quickly not only fail to grind but are also chipped or bruised.

After the tumbler has been going about 10 days, add another 3 oz. of 80 grit silicon carbide. How long this first grinding will now take depends on several factors, of which the roughness and toughness of the material being tumbled are the most decisive. When the shapes of all the stones are well rounded, it is time to go on to finer grinding.

All the 80 grit silicon carbide and any pieces of broken grinding wheel must now be washed out of both the stones and the tumbling barrel. They need not be thrown away however (and certainly should not be allowed to go down the sink) but can be strained in a cloth and kept for re-use.

Discard any damaged stones and wash the rest thoroughly in a mixture of warm water and detergent. Tumbling the stones in suds for a few minutes is as good a way as any. Hobbyists using containers such as discarded paint cans should keep a special can for each stage of tumbling because of the difficulty of ensuring that the can is washed free of grit.

The washed stones are loaded back into the tumbling barrel, again covered with water and 3 to 4 oz. of 320 grit silicon carbide added. Tumbling in this mixture should go on about a week, not forgetting to burp the barrel regularly.

Repeat the washing procedure and discard any damaged stones. Refill the barrel with stones, water and 2 to 3 oz. of 500 grit silicon carbide. Tumbling is continued, again for about a week. By this time all the stones should be quite smooth, showing a matt finish.

It is advisable to keep a spare barrel specially for polishing so that no contamination with grit can occur. Extra care should also be taken when washing the stones before polishing.

Now a new ingredient is added to the mixture in the polishing barrel.

This is called buffer material and we include it to prevent the stones damaging each other as they polish. The buffer can be masonite chips, shredded leather, wood chips or plastic granules, although the last-named are the most convenient to use.

The polishing agent is about 3 oz. of either cerium oxide or tin oxide to which is added two or three teaspoonsful of soap flakes with enough water to cover the load. After a couple of days the stones should be showing a brilliant lustre. Check this by examining a selection of them under a strong light. If they show reflections sharp and clear as a mirror, we may be satisfied with the polish.

Stop the tumbler, empty the barrel, rinse the stones clean and spread them on a cloth to dry. Both the plastic granules and the polishing powder can be recovered for further use.

If the desired polish has not been attained after three days, rinse the contents of the barrel and go through the process again. Bruised stones will have to be reground with 500 grit before the second polish. Stones showing undercutting are best discarded.

Glassy stones such as obsidian, goldstone and the crystalline quartz varieties give better results if they are tumbled for about a week in a mixture of 3 to 4 oz. of pumice powder before polishing. Plastic granules or some other buffer agent should be used at each stage of grinding as well as polishing but new material should be substituted for the final polish to prevent contamination.

Buffers should also be used with petalite, amazonite, aragonite, rhodonite and rhodochrosite. In the case of amazonite, aragonite, rhodochrosite and similar soft stones, grinding should be started at 220 grit, rising to 400 and 600. Tiger's-eye can be damaged by tumbling too quickly at the coarse grinding stage. Reducing the speed of the tumbler and spending more time on each process are good tactics with all these stones.

It is always a mistake to imagine that tumbling can be carried out to a timetable. Periods of time given in instructions such as these are merely a guide. The factor which decides the length of time each process must take is the condition of the stones themselves. So long as any roughness persists, coarse grinding should continue. Each finer stage of grinding must remove the marks left by the stage before it. Continued too long, polishing can spoil the finish of stones rather than improve it.

We should strive for 100 per cent perfection from our tumbling machine although we can never expect to achieve it. There will always be stones that for one reason or another do not match the best of the batch. These stones should be reserved for further treatment or for less important uses. Only the very best should be made up as costume jewellery.

Lapidary dealers' catalogues disclose an increasing number of well-designed settings for every kind of jewellery on offer to hobby gemworkers. No doubt some of the former clumsy, cheap-looking stuff is still around, but new graceful shapes in sterling silver and 9 carat gold are sweeping it out of sight. But the setting need not be silver or gold; gilding metal or German silver can look equally good providing the design is right. In matching our tumbled gemstones to their settings, a special quality is needed—good taste.

Good taste is the referee in our own minds who draws the line between what looks attractive, stylish and original and what looks merely silly and vulgar. If we are fortunate enough to have the kind of good taste that approximates to the average, our matching of stones and settings will prove popular. If not, we can at least profit by experience.

It is good taste plus imagination which decides whether a gold or silver setting is needed for a particular stone. Obsidians and deep blue sodalite are popularly accepted as looking their best against silver, but cherry-red jasper, opalite and prase can be effective, too.

Always the setting should enhance the best qualities of the stone, displaying the translucent and transparent gems to the light and acting as a foil to the rich colours of opaque stones.

Have these thoughts in mind as you browse through the dealers' catalogue and make your selection. Tumbled stones can be made into brooches and pendants, earrings and cuff-links as well as their traditionally popular roles as bracelets or necklets and ornaments for key rings.

In most cases, the stone is glued directly to the setting with an epoxy jewellers' cement, but in some bracelets and pendants, one or more stones are secured to chains by means of jewellers' findings known as jump rings and bell caps. Other findings include spring bails, bolt rings, fold-over and barrel clasps. Apart from rolled gold and silver, the popular finish for findings is plating with rhodium, a whitish-grey member of the platinum family.

Bell caps are star-shaped findings with a little ring in the centre of the star and from two to seven so-called fingers. A variety of sizes is available. Jewellers' pliers are needed to bend the fingers and shape the caps so that they can be cemented to the stones. As epoxy cement has to stand in warm air for a while before it becomes rock-hard, some people use trays of sand to hold the stones upright during the interval. However, a dab of Plasticine under each stone is equally effective and more convenient.

Brooches and pendants are so often made with tumbled stones to have become rather hackneyed, but the answer is to look for the findings that have new ideas and better quality. Now the range of bought settings for baroque jewellery has been extended to include almost every imaginable item—rings, earrings, tie-clips and tie-tacks, even cuff-links—and more novelty ideas are coming along all the time. There is even a setting in pliable metal which can be bent into the shape of any tumbled stone.

Stones with interesting markings or inclusions can be made into fob brooches by means of bell caps, jump rings and bow pins, either in rolled gold or sterling silver. Findings for souvenir jewellery include boomerangs and maps of Australia which can be set with opal chips or small fragments of other Australian-produced gems such as chrysoprase or rhodonite.

Properly tumbled gemstones deserve settings to match their beauty. Once this happy union has been achieved, the result is not the poor relation of any other kind of jewellery, but fine jewellery in its own right.

Most of the settings and findings illustrated elsewhere are shown by courtesy of Mr. Elio Re, of Australian Lapidary Supplies. However, the vast majority of lapidary suppliers, now numerous throughout Australia, can offer a wide range of high quality items.

## COSTS

Prices of the tumbling machines mentioned in this chapter at the end of 1966, were: Thompson Lapidary Supplies' light duty tumbler (without motor) $13. Gemmasta tumbling machine (less barrel and motor) $24; barrels (6 lb., 3 lb., 1 lb.) $13, $7, $5.50 extra respectively. R. L. and W. P. Hall's tumbler unit, with two quart containers and 60 watt motor, $35. Jack Taylor's Mighty Mite (with motor, containers, grits and polishes) $35.70 (standard); $37.80 (de luxe); Multi-Mite, $40. Australian Lapidary Supplies tumbler M11-1 (without motor) $5.95. The Galaxy tumbling barrel costs $5.25. Postage and packing charges are not included.

Small findings such as bell caps, jump rings, bolt rings and spring bails, either gilt or silver, rhodium-plated, sterling silver, rolled gold, 9 carat gold and some in copper are mostly sold by the dozen or the gross, although bolt rings, bails and clasps may be bought individually. Bell caps, 22c. to $2.25 a doz.; jump rings, 7 cents to 75 cents a doz. Sterling silver, rhodium-plated or rolled gold chain is sold by the foot ranging from 5 cents to $4.50, or in 50 ft. and 100 ft. lengths. Prices of settings and mountings for pendants, brooches, earrings, rings, tie-pins and tie-tacks, bracelets, cuff-links and key-rings in all these metals range from nearly $13 to a few cents according to size and composition.

Jewellery pliers, $1.25 and $1.60 a pair; sufficient epoxy cement to mount 200 bell caps costs 50 cents.

These prices are, of course, subject to fluctuation and are not binding on any lapidary dealer.

# 3

# ECONOMIC EQUIPMENT

## by Jack S. Taylor

Only a fraction of the people active in the lapidary hobby have their own workrooms. I have been told that this fraction is about a quarter and I see no reason to doubt it. There are a variety of reasons why people who enjoy working with gemstones are reluctant to set up their own equipment.

Before tackling the main points, let us deal with a couple of minor misconceptions. First of all, those couples with young families who are worried about having machinery about the place. Fears for young children should not stop anyone from setting up a workroom providing they are prepared to take a few sensible precautions.

Moving belts are dangerous of course, and measures have to be taken to keep children away from them. Switches must be placed out of reach and so on. But the lapidary machines themselves are quite harmless. People get a shock when they see me put my finger on the edge of a diamond saw while the blade is whizzing round. Afterwards they are surprised to see the finger is still there and not even cut.

The only things that might do a bit of damage are the grinding wheels. If a child puts its fingers on one of them while the wheel is moving, it might take the skin off, but that's all. On the other hand, children can do little damage to lapidary equipment. About the worst they could manage would be to contaminate it by getting the abrasive grits mixed with the polish. But that's nothing that couldn't be put right easily.

Some people hesitate to instal lapidary machinery because they think it will make a lot of noise or annoy the neighbours in some other way. In fact this problem rarely arises with modern, well-designed equipment that has been properly manufactured. Then they fear this must be very costly—and, of course, this is one of the main reasons why people do not set up their own workrooms. But this is not so if they are prepared to buy wisely and obtain machines suited to their particular needs.

It all depends on how people go about it. If they want something really elaborate, then they will spend a lot of money. I have friends who are so keen on the hobby that they want to buy all the equipment and have everything. Well, that costs plenty. But that does not mean that anyone who is unable to spend on the same scale cannot buy more modest equipment and do excellent work.

Providing you buy good quality machinery, you can build up a workroom by degrees. A well-made machine will last for years and is the cheapest in the long run. My advice to anyone who wants to buy equipment but is a bit short of chips is to buy the basic items but be sure that what you buy is sound and solid, with ball bearings instead of ordinary bearings and so on.

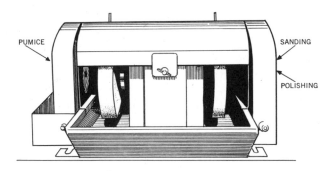

*Jack Taylor offers this compact unit for the hobby gemworker short of space. Grinding, sanding and polishing can all be done in an area less than half a square yard.*

Let me illustrate what I call buying with an eye to the future. Take two similar machines, say a double-ended grinding head. Both are equipped with six-inch silicon carbide wheels, but the one that costs a little bit more is fitted with guards and bearings that can take eight-inch wheels. The other, for cheapness, is scaled down to take only six-inch.

Which one do you buy? For my money the dearest one is the cheapest. Six-inch grinding wheels are little more than toys and you will soon wear them out. By then you will want to advance to more professional equipment and do better work. That means eight-inch wheels and unless your grinder is equipped to take them, you cannot do this without buying a completely new machine.

The other big problem is housing. People think lapidary equipment needs a lot of space. This is quite wrong. As time goes on they will realise that they can do very good work with small equipment. Because they realise that space is such a problem, manufacturers have devised a great variety of combination units that enable you to carry out three or four operations on a bench area little greater than that required for one machine.

As an example you see illustrated a little machine of mine that is typical of this type of unit. It offers all the essentials—a double grinder, a sander and a polisher—and at the same time it has been designed in such a way that you can't get contamination from grits on the polisher. A machine of this type is the best and cheapest with which to start.

Both the rough grinder and the fine grinder are well shielded. There is no dust coming from them. Water dripping on the wheels from above ensures that all grit goes straight into the tray. When you have finished grinding, you attach your sanding disc in the place provided on the right-hand end. After sanding is done, you switch over to the left side for your pumice. All this time your final polishing felt with its guard is still on the shelf well out of the way of any contamination.

Nothing from the sander is going to go right round the machine to get on the pumice wheel. It would have to travel 2 ft. 6 in. as well as turn a corner. In the same way nothing from the pumice wheel can reach your felt buff. Only after you have finished with the pumice and washed both your hands and your stone is it time to replace the sanding disc with the polisher.

As long as the person using it observes commonsense rules of cleanliness and keeps his hands out of the grit in the trays, there is less risk of contamination with a properly designed combination unit than separate machines. After all, bad workroom layout can result from grits on the grinder or the sander being blown on to the polishing buffs. With this unit that cannot happen.

Of course a combination unit has to be equipped to operate at two or more speeds. A diamond saw (where one is included) operates at between 2000 and 3000 revolutions a minute and grinding wheels at between 1400 and 2000, while sanders and polishers are run much more slowly at about 350 r.p.m. Therefore the unit has to be provided with different diameter pulleys to give these various speeds.

That is the basic set-up. Anybody who wants to go a bit better can fit the machine with a couple of different grade sanders at either end and mount the pumice and final polisher separately on a slower-running double head.

Once you have separate units, you are faced with the problem of providing power in two places, although not necessarily at the same time unless two people are using the equipment. The most economical way of doing this is a motor mount, which is a sort of cradle that allows your power unit to be moved around and clipped in place on any machine where it is needed.

Is a diamond saw a luxury or a necessity? The answer to that one depends on whether you have the money to buy it or not. Possessing a saw is certainly a great convenience. Up to a 10-inch saw is quite good enough for the amateur who only wants to do small slabbing and trimming on it. Over that size, it's really not a trim saw.

The man who goes out and collects big hunks of rock has either got to equip himself with a saw of 20-inch or so diameter (which will cost $600 or $700) or take it to a dealer who will slab it for him at a charge of 10 cents or so a square inch. But even the man who has only a 6 in. saw can cut through beach pebbles if he rigs up some kind of clamp to hold the pebble rigid while it is cut.

Whatever the size of saw, it must have a good blade. A lot of people have this idea that a good blade must be a very thin blade. This is another fallacy. The thinner the saw blade, the more likely it is to get damaged. The only people who need an extra thin blade are those who are working in opal. The best sort to buy is the general purpose diamond-impregnated blade, that is segmented all round the periphery and you don't have to charge with diamond dust yourself.

Some people think that for cheapness they can buy diamond dust and roll it into their saw blade themselves. They forget that they will have to keep on charging and charging it. It's much better to buy the ready-charged blade that lasts far longer. Even these blades cost only a tenth of the price of the bonded or sintered blades which last many years. But bonded blades are very expensive.

The whole question of how to equip a workroom depends on individual preferences and ambitions. If a person wants to go in for lapidary in a big way, he will want a whole range of expensive machinery and a special room in which to fit it up. If you have the space and the money, that's all right. But you can still do all the work you like, if you can only afford a combination unit—a grinder/sander/polisher say, with a little saw alongside it.

So long as you keep it clean, you can fit all that easily into a 6 ft. x 6 ft. room. But if you have a 16 ft. x 16 ft. room to spare or a couple of rooms or a big shed out at the back, you can do things on a bigger scale. It all depends on the facilities available. If you have to build, even a prefabricated place is going to put up your costs considerably. However, most people find they can fit in all the equipment they need on a bench at the back of the garage.

Wherever you are working, you will need electric power points. Any new points necessary must be installed by a qualified electrician, just as you have to get a licensed plumber to lay on mains water supplies. Make sure that all your electrical gear is safe, using heavy duty cable with your ¼ h.p. motor and never on any account running your machines off electric light sockets.

You also must have an ample water supply although this need be no more than a tank on the wall running down to a bucket under your machine. But water at mains pressure will splash back at you and before very long you'll be wet through and working in a pool of water.

Ordinary mains pressure is too great. It's better to buy an old cistern or one of those small galvanised tanks the type they use on chicken farms that keeps filling itself from the mains and won't overflow. With a set-up of that kind, you will have a supply of water at low pressure, which is just what you need.

A constant supply of water is necessary when grinding, of course, to cool and lubricate the stone. Grinding wheels are made of silicon carbide grits bonded with clay and other ingredients. The grit size and hardness is usually marked in code on the label of the wheel. Hardness is expressed as a letter of the alphabet ranging from A for very soft to Z for very hard while the grit size is expressed as the amount of mesh to the inch through which it would pass.

Basic needs for grinding are a coarse wheel and a fine wheel. For average stones, a 100 and a 220 grit are quite good enough and a variety of sanders will supply all you need apart from that. If you are cutting opal or other soft stones such as malachite or turquoise, a 200 and a 320 grit is a better combination. If you are cutting everything, fit up a 320 wheel as well as the 100 and the 220.

The usual range of sanding cloths is 220, 320, 400, 500 and 600. Personally I use cloth discs with peel-off cement. You have a sponge rubber disc cemented on to the wheel with contact adhesive. The required grade of silicon carbide cloth is stuck to the rubber with peel-off cement and all you have to do if you want to substitute another grade is peel it off. You must have the little bit of roundness provided by the sponge rubber.

A disc sander is cheaper, less trouble and easier to work than the drum or belt sander. The disc sander also provides a range of working speeds from the edge to the centre while the drum sander has only one.

A new idea developing in Australia is to use four or five different grades of sanding instead of pumice, which many amateurs dislike. When I was in Hobart and Brisbane recently I found the local club members using 320, 400, 500 and 600 sandpapers and no pumice.

Strangely enough, when I first started years ago, we never used a sander. My first cutting was done on the flat with a lead wheel and two grades of silicon carbide grit, coarse and fine. For sanding we just used to use the slurry at the side of the wheel. Then we went on for a quick lick of the pumice, then on the tin oxide buff and finish.

Now sandpaper is doing away with the pumice and a new technique has been evolved. As long as you learn the basic principles of lapidary, there is always room to try out different techniques and if you find one that gives better results, by all means change to it. There's the basic principle to follow but you can always go by either side of the road to attain your final finish and do it an easier way if you can.

However with this one there is that little risk of the sandpaper getting too hot and damaging your stone. You don't have that risk with pumice because it is wet and I was taught to always keep the stone wet.

It must be admitted that pumice is probably the most common cause of contamination. Once pumice gets on a polishing wheel it is impossible to achieve a brilliant finish. Watch out for getting pumice under your finger nails, in the cracks of stones, on dopsticks and especially on your apron. Beware wiping the stone on your apron because it is only too easy to feed back the pumice on to the polishing wheels.

Polishing offers the greatest variety of techniques than any process. The other day I had a chap come along who was trying to polish a piece of New Zealand greenstone. He said it wouldn't polish on felt. I suggested he use leather and made him up a special lap. Later on he came back and said: "This stuff won't polish." I said it would and eventually bet him a fiver that not only could I polish it but that I could polish it on felt.

I took the stone on the felt wheel and in two minutes it was polished. His eyes nearly popped out of his head. It was just a matter of technique. I had used the felt all right but instead of keeping it wet—his mistake had been keeping it too wet—I had let it dry out and used a controlled molecular flow to polish it as the stone grew hot.

He didn't know anything about molecular flow. No amateur can expect to learn in six months what it takes a professional six years to learn. As a technique using the dry polisher has its dangers and if you're not careful you can easily damage your stone.

I do most of my polishing on felt but sometimes I strike a rare stone where I have to go on to leather. Leather is good if ever you have trouble with soft stones.

One or two of the compact machines have flat laps for cutting cabochons and faceting on a single "pot-type" machine. Amateurs seem to find cutting cabochons difficult on a flat lap, however. They like to watch their stone and find this is easier on the vertical wheels.

Personally I prefer cutting on a flat lap, perhaps because I was taught to cut stones that way. On a flat lap you have a better control of speed —slower on the edge, faster towards the centre.

One advantage of these flat lap machines is that they cut down contamination risks even when cutting cabochons. When you change wheels, you put away the one you have been using, wipe the splash-bowl clean and put on the new wheel. As long as your hands and stone are clean, there can't be any contamination.

The risks are even less in faceting because there are only two processes, cutting and polishing, compared to five or six for cabochons. You can't polish until you've finished cutting. Then you have to change the lap, so you clean everything up.

Although there is now a large and increasing demand for faceting heads, faceting is still a mystery to many amateurs and they imagine it is very difficult. So it is in one or two details. You have to concentrate and you have to work some very fine touches on the little facets. But, broadly speaking, with modern aids faceting is not that difficult.

When I learnt faceting, I had to cut those little facets by feel and I had to go all round the stone by feel. There was no mechanical means of doing it then. We used a jamb peg, a kind of inverted cone of hardwood with graduated and angled holes into which the end of the dopstick was placed.

When you wanted to cut a facet you did it by eye and your finger was on the opposite side and you had to gauge it by touch. You had to guess how long to cut because there was no stop such as the modern mechanical faceting heads possess to prevent you over-cutting.

But these modern heads can be set to angles and indexed on which facets to cut first and a chart tells you that you have to cut quartz a little differently than zircon and sapphire in another way and so on. True you have to know the order of the facets and the angles to which they must be set but you soon learn those.

Faceting heads sold in Australia are of two types, the freehand and the fixed index head. The first-named is not as expensive as the fixed index head. Another type in some ways similar to the freehand head is the mechanical dopstick. You can only do squares and rounds with these whereas you can cut more complicated stones such as hexagonals and ovals with the fixed index heads.

Using these heads amateurs can soon facet gemstones like zircons, amethysts and the other quartz gems and they get on to sapphires quite quickly. It's not hard but it gets more difficult when you start trying fancy shapes like ovals and pendeloques. Probably the amateur would have to get a very expensive mechanical head indeed before he could tackle those.

But with ordinary cheap devices like the freehand head and the mechanical dopstick it is possible to enjoy faceting and do very good work. Perhaps it would be difficult to some people, just as playing the violin or the guitar is difficult to some people while others who have the ability can pick it up very easily.

I think these cheaper faceting heads will give you more fun than the more expensive ones. But many amateurs have got it fixed in their minds that because the angles are all preset and they only have to turn the knobs, that the fixed index heads are so much easier.

Before you can start faceting, you've got to have a good cutting wheel. A copper lap with a cutting grade of diamond dust rolled into it is the popular one and in this case I would say it is the best. You can also use a cast steel lap with silicon carbide grits or even a silicon carbide wheel but they are not the best. They wear quickly and have to be trued with a diamond dresser.

Polishing laps vary according to the stones being cut. You've got to have a copper lap with tripoli for sapphires and the lap will have to be scored, or hacked as we say, to hold the powder. For quartz you use cerium oxide on a plastic lap. If you can't get lucite, an old gramophone record is quite good and it already has grooves on it to hold the polish.

American gem-cutters prefer very fine diamond dust for polishing. They use a polishing grade of dust on a copper lap for a wide range of stones. Personally I prefer the old German or English methods; they cut on diamond dust, but they polish on all the different agents. You get a polish all right with the diamond dust, but you get a super polish the other way.

I know an Australian sapphire-cutter, one of our best, who cuts with diamond on copper and also uses the very fine dust on copper for polishing. But when he has finished that and cleaned his stone, he goes over it again quickly on the copper and tripoli. He uses diamond dust for quickness but he relies on the old methods to get that better polish.

Different styles of gem carving call for different tools. Overseas they still use the German method of a lathe on which they mount little tools, points and wheels charged with abrasive. Then they hold the gem they're carving and move it against the tool. That's the way they have been carving for hundreds of years.

The new method is to use a flexible drill like a dentist's drill and grind the stone away with the point of it. That's getting very much like the sculptor who chips away at a block of stone. With the drill you just change the tips for sanding, smoothing and polishing. All those little tips are available from the shops now, but the main thing is to get a good flexible shaft. The cheap ones often have too much play and cause too much vibration to be of much use for carving. You might have to pay $80 or $100 for a good shaft but then they are on ball bearings and don't get hot in use.

Another thing to watch is that the little tools and fittings are often on an eighth-inch shank, while the dentist's drills are $\frac{5}{32}$s or $\frac{3}{32}$s in the spindle. So when you buy a hand piece, get one that has a sort of a chuck and is adaptable to all the different sizes.

Ingenuity is the hall-mark of the successful gem-carver and he makes his own little tools quite cheaply. With a wad punch, for instance, you can stamp out little felt wheels about an inch in diameter or circles of tinplate the same size to make little saw blades or tiny lead wheels for cutting with grits. Other points and cutting tools can be fashioned from silicon carbide blocks.

What future trends do I see for lapidary in Australia? Well, I expect we shall see more people taking up faceting, but even more taking an interest in one or other of the various forms of gem-carving. I don't imagine that the new vibratory devices now coming in will make very much difference.

The new vibratory lap is a beauty for cutting flat surfaces, but it is no good for little slabs or for finishing cabochons. It's only for the big chunks of minerals and so on, where you want to prepare a specimen piece and this lap does a wonderful job on that. It's a real boon to the mineral collector but it's hard to see how it can affect gem-cutting.

## COSTS

Jack Taylor's grinder/sander/polisher, 6 in. wheels, $41; 8 in. wheels, $48. Gemmasta 6 in. saw/grinder/sander/polisher, $116; junior unit, $4\frac{3}{8}$ in. saw, 5 in. wheels, $69.50; grinder/sander/polisher (less wheels) 6 in., $64; 8 in., $70; 10 in., $95; belt sander, $136. Robilt 6 in. saw/grinder/sander/polisher, $85. Junior Gem-Maker, 6 in. saw/grinder/sander/polisher, $40; Thompson's 10 in. saw/grinder/sander/polisher, $230; 8 in. grinder/sander/polis'er, $90 to $104.

Hall's 6 in. grinder/sander/polisher, $60; 8 in., $80. Agatemaster 6 in. saw/grinder/sander/polisher, $125; bare (but with discs) $100; 8 in. (no motor) $198; bare, $150. Wormald 6 in. grinder/polisher, complete, $34.50. Little Jewel 6 in. grinder/polisher, $50; 8 in., $75; with saw, $115.

Taylor's 10 in. slabbing/trim saw, $120. Robilt 10 in. slab/trim saw, $120; 6 in. trim saw, $40. Thompson's 10 in. slab/trim saw, $117.50; 16-20 in. slab saw (motorised, less blade) $600; 24 in. slab saw (motorised, less blade) $680. Gemmasta 6 in. trim saw (less blade) $48; 10 in. trim/slab saw (less blade) $95. Hall's 8 in. trim saw, $54; 8 in. slab/trim saw, $60 to $80; 10 in. slab/trim saw, $106, all with blades; 12-16 in. (less blade) $240. Agatemaster 12 in. slab saw, weight feed, $170; power feed, $210, blade and motor extra; 6 in. trim saw, $49; 8 in. with vice, $95, no motor. Minex 8 in. trim saw (with blade) $60. Diaboart 10 in. slab/trim saw, $120. Diamond saw blades, 4 in. $11.65 to 24 in. $92.

Taylor's Little Gem, 6 in. saw/6 in. wheels/cabochon/faceting unit, complete $90; 8 in. wheels, $95. Robilt Gem Maker, 6 in. saw/cabochon/faceting unit, complete, $67.50. Hall's flat lap, with accessories, $49.55.

Motors, second-hand, $5.50 to $15; new, ¼ h.p., $27 to $31; 1/3 h.p., $31.50 to $35; ½ h.p., $34.50 to $42.50. Motor bars (for mobility) $1.75; supports, 75 cents. Postage and packing charges not included.

These prices are as quoted at the end of 1966, and are subject to fluctuation. They are not binding on any lapidary machine manufacturer or dealer.

# 4

# SHINING STONES

## by Lloyd Meller

THE FIRST STEP in cutting and polishing a cabochon is to select the right stone. Preferably, this will be one that is not too high on the scale of hardness, free from flaws and capable of taking a good polish.

Although flowering obsidian, opalite or goldstone do not fill all these requirements, any one of them makes a good first choice. All possess the advantage that the outline of the cabochon may be marked on either side of the slab, and, should any errors occur in cutting, the size of the stone can be reduced without greatly affecting the pattern.

Before starting work, make a check on necessary tools and equipment. First in order of use are the jeweller's eyepiece or magnifying glass and an apron. Then a marking pencil (aluminium for preference, but a brass one is handy for light-coloured stones) and a template giving various cabochon shapes in standard sizes.

Three or four dopsticks are needed, each made from a length of quarter-inch dowel rod and tapered at one end. Dopsticks should be about half an inch less in length than the distance between the centre of the grinding wheel and the board or tray on which the grinding head rests.

Other dopping requirements are a small spirit lamp, a butcher's knife, a stick of red china wax, a pair of five or six-inch tweezers with rounded ends and a piece of wood 8 in. by 4 in. by ¾ in. with several holes drilled in it to hold the tapered ends of the dopsticks.

Necessary tools on the bench are a grinding head with two silicon carbide grinding wheels, 100 grit on the left and a 220 grit on the right-hand side; two silicon carbide disc sanders, a 320 and a 500; a pumice wheel; a putty wheel and a leather wheel. Extras such as a 320 grit wheel, a wider range of sanders and special buffs can wait until later on.

The grinding head is fitted with 6 or 8 in. wheels with a 1 in. face. Running speed is about 2,000 revolutions a minute. The 100 grit wheel is for rough shaping and the 220 wheel for finish shaping. Usually soft bonded wheels are used, such as 37CJV, as it is necessary for the wheel to wear a certain amount to expose new sharp particles of grit to ensure efficient cutting.

It is also necessary to have water running on the wheel's cutting face to keep heat down to a minimum and to carry away grinding debris and so prevent the wheel becoming clogged. As grinding wheels are extremely porous, they readily absorb water while stationary, thereby becoming unbalanced and dangerous. For this reason it is essential that the lapidary switch on the power to the wheels before he turns the water tap on, and conversely, turn the water off before the power is switched off. Make sure the hands are quite dry before touching the switch.

Another safety factor worth remembering is that such articles of clothing as ties and scarves should never be worn loose near drive belts or pulley wheels.

The 320 and 500 grit sanders consist of two 8 in. silicon carbide cloth discs backed by a $\frac{3}{16}$ in. or $\frac{1}{4}$ in. layer of sponge rubber so that when the dopped stone is pressed against the disc, a certain amount of cushioning permits a greater portion of the sander to smooth the stone.

The pumice wheel is a hard felt 8 in. wheel which is charged with a slurry of pumice powder and water. Tripoli powder also may be used.

The putty wheel is of a softer 8 in. felt. One to two teaspoons of tin oxide to a pint jar of water is the usual mixture.

Running speeds for sander, pumice, putty and leather wheels should be 350-400 r.p.m.

Having made a choice from obsidian, opalite or goldstone, the beginner will do well to start on a simple cabochon in an oval shape, preferably a 30 x 40 millimetre size. It is far easier to hold a stone of this size against a fast spinning wheel with both hands than a smaller one, say of 18 x 25 mm. size.

The template is placed over the stone and the oval shape is marked out on the slab avoiding flaws and selecting the area with the most colourful and attractive pattern. Angle the marking pencil with the point directed towards the rim of the template oval rather than perpendicularly or towards the centre of the oval.

The slab is now taken to the 100 grit wheel for removal of excess material. This is an appropriate time to consider the desirability of nibbling. Nibbling is the removal of excess material by the use of end-cutter pincers. Unless the pincers are used carefully and where little risk exists of breaking into that part of the stone inside the marked oval, nibbling should be avoided.

However, pincers can be used to advantage in preparing slabbed material selected for tumbling before trimming on the rough grinding wheel. Similar pincers are used extensively on the opal fields for snipping opal nobbies to assess colour.

Often slabs of goldstone, opalite or obsidian are rough ground on the 220 wheel but providing the wheel face is well trimmed and careful attention paid to the pressure used, any of the three can be worked quite satisfactorily on a 100 grit wheel.

Held in both hands and in a horizontal position on the same level as the axle or spindle on which the wheels are mounted, the slab is very slowly rotated in a clockwise or anti-clockwise direction as it is carefully ground down to within $\frac{1}{32}$ in. of the inscribed oval line.

Should the wheel chip the stone too much, either ease the pressure being applied or turn the stone to a perpendicular position so that it is in the same plane as the wheel itself, and slowly turn it end over end as it is presented to the wheel. In this event, it will be necssary to check the depth of cutting constantly, or lean a little to the left so that the rate at which material is being removed can be seen.

Having now ground the slab to the predetermined margin from the line, now turn to the opposite side to that with the marked oval (the back of the stone) and make three distinct cuts around the stone until it is roughly domed.

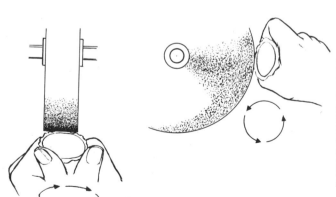

*The marked slab, held in both hands, is rough ground to within $\frac{1}{32}$ of an inch of the template outline. Should it chip, the stone can be turned edge on to the grinding wheel. In either case it should be slowly revolved.*

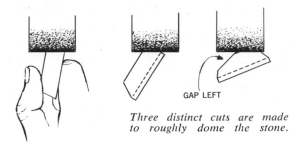

*Three distinct cuts are made
to roughly dome the stone.*

To achieve the angle of the first cut, stand just slightly to the left of the centre of the wheel and present the edge of the stone to the wheel by holding it between the middle fingers of each hand and slowly turning it end over end with the right thumb until the uniformity of cut is attained. The second and third cuts are done in a similar way, only moving a little further left and towards the machine on each occasion.

As soon as the top of the stone is roughly shaped, it is ready for dopping, which is the attaching of the stone to a dopstick by means of a special wax.

Ability to do a good dop has a marked effect on the overall quality of the work produced and this ability is best obtained by practice.

Red china wax is the best type to use. The dopstick is held by the tapered end in one hand whilst the wax is held in the other and heated over the spirit lamp until it becomes soft. The soft wax is then wiped on to the end of the dopstick. After three or four pieces of wax have adhered to the dopstick, take the butcher's knife in the left hand, either butting the tip of the blade into or laying it on the bench, and proceed to alternately heat the wax and roll it down the knife towards the tip.

When held over the flame the waxed dopstick should be rolled back and forth so that the wax around the stick is warmed evenly and not just in one spot. Keep adding more wax to the dopstick until there is sufficient wax on the stick to attach a stone to the top. The finished dop should be smooth and neatly tapered.

The rough shaped stone is now dopped with the flat side (back) uppermost so that the exact finished outline of the base can be cut and the setting edge positioned. With the stone held by a pair of long tweezers, alternately heat the stone and the wax dop. The stone and the wax should be touched together every few seconds or so, and when it is noticed that some of the wax has stuck to the stone, it will then be ready to dop.

Quickly place the stone on the bench, flat side down, press the wax on to the stone and work it around the stone neatly with moistened fingers.

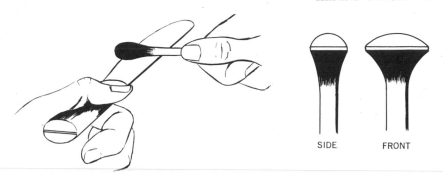

*Dopping wax is rolled onto the dopstick by means of a knife blade. The wax is smoothed and neatly tapered to the shape of the stone.*

It may be necessary to place the stone and the dop over the lamp and reheat the wax where it has not formed a good bond and rework the wax with the fingers.

The fact that the stone is secure on the stick is not by any means sufficient for a good dop. The following points must also be observed:

1. In a 30 x 40 cabochon, dopped dome uppermost, the edge of the wax should not come closer than $\frac{1}{16}$ of an inch to the outline of the surface to which it is attached so that it is possible later to silhouette the stone to the light to check for symmetry of shape.

If the wax is allowed to overlap the edge of any stone, it will give a false reading on the outline. It will also clog the grinding wheel or the sander or contaminate the polishing buffs.

2. The stone must be in the centre of the dopstick so that it is well balanced.

3. When viewed from any quarter, the stone must be at right angles to the dopstick for subsequent accurate cutting.

4. The wax surface and the join with the stone must be smooth and free from cracks or holes so that sander grit or pumice are not carried on to the polishing buffs even after hands and dopped stone have been washed.

After constant use, even the most carefully made dop can lose its adhesiveness by absorbing impurities, and it is a good policy to add a little fresh wax once in a while.

If difficulty is experienced in keeping a stone on the dop in cold weather, a little flake shellac can be added. The best way to do this is to soften the wax on the dopstick over the lamp and dip the dop into the jar of flake shellac, reheat over the lamp and roll the adhering flakes of shellac into the wax. One dip of shellac is usually enough. Shellac hardens the wax and raises the melting point.

Pitch is also used for dops particularly if shellac is used as a jointing compound for doublets as it has a lower melting point than the shellac. The dopstick is charged with pitch in exactly the same way as with wax.

With the stone satisfactorily dopped, the first step is to cut the outside edge of the stone down to its exact and final outline. Incidentally, if ever you get impatient to finish a stone quickly, always remember that lapidary work is a hobby in which one hurries *SLOWLY* if perfect work is the ultimate aim. If too much of the stone is cut away, it cannot be put back again.

From now on, all grinding is done on the 220 grit wheel. Holding the dopstick perpendicularly in both hands, the stone in a horizontal position is now brought into contact with the face of the wheel on the same plane as the shaft on which the wheel spins. It is this process which determines the maximum length of the dopstick (mentioned earlier) and at this stage it is often necessary to shorten dopsticks.

If the stone is worked on the wheel at a point lower than the shaft it will not be possible to ascertain the true outline of the base of the stone. The same error will occur if the dopstick is not held perpendicularly.

Slowly turn the dopped stone in an anti-clockwise direction two or

*The dopped stone should be ground at the same level as the shaft of the grinding wheel and rotated in both directions alternately. Otherwise it will develop the faults shown on the right.*

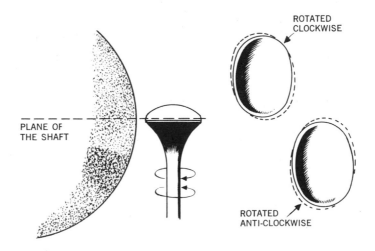

PLANE OF
THE SHAFT

ROTATED
CLOCKWISE

ROTATED
ANTI-CLOCKWISE

three times, then reverse to clockwise. If the direction of cutting is not changed there is a tendency for the stone to be unsymmetrical in shape on the adjacent points of the oval. This is a very common fault.

It is possible to cut the stone at this stage with the slab in the same plane as the wheel with the dopstick parallel to the spindle shaft, but this method does not allow sufficient accuracy and the possibility of cutting through the marked line demands more constant checking.

This stage is completed when the outline of the stone is cut down on to—but not through—the line. If the stone is to be mounted in a finding, it should be constantly checked during this process until the exact fit is obtained.

If there is some doubt as to the exact symmetry of shape, a quick and simple test will readily disclose any irregularity. Hold the stone at arm's length with the tapered end of the dopstick pointed away from the body, and silhouette the oval outline against the light. Keeping the eye on the suspected irregularity, rotate the stone quickly through 180 degrees so that a comparison is made with the opposite side. By repeating this once or twice it will soon be obvious where the irregularity is and the necessary adjustment can be made.

It is good practice to include this check of comparing one end against the other and one side against the other in the normal process of cutting as the stone is being brought down to the finished shape. It is a mistake to rely on every template being accurate as far as symmetry of shape is concerned and this point should be checked when buying one.

The exact shape having been attained, it is now necessary to put a setting edge on the stone which will facilitate setting it in a bezel and also give the stone greater strength when the bezel is being worked to fit it. The setting edge also allows a polished stone to be picked up more easily from a flat surface.

The setting edge is cut on the back by turning the stone around at an angle of 45 degrees, preferably on the side of the wheel, if the equipment has provision for a water jet to the side. The cutting rate is much slower on the side and after all very little has to be removed. Cutting can also be done quite satisfactorily on the face of the wheel. The stone should be turned completely round against the wheel before being lifted so that the depth of cut will be uniform. Two or three light turns of the stone are usually sufficient.

Should the stone be polished on the back? Generally speaking, a stone unpolished on the back is regarded as not being completed. However, if the stone is to be mounted in such a way that the back will not be seen when worn, then it seems to be wasted effort. Should the stone be cemented in a standard mount, adhesion would be much better to an unpolished surface than to one which had been polished.

On the other hand, transparent or translucent stones can be polished at the back to increase the passage of light and enhance their beauty, while anyone intending to display the stone in competition must polish the back of it irrespective of the type of material from which it is cut.

On the assumption that the stone on which you are working is to be mounted and the back unseen, it will now be removed from the dop and redopped the other way up.

There are two main ways of removing a stone from the dop. The first employs the butcher's knife. Keep a firm pressure on the knife so that the curve of the blade is in contact with the bench at all times. Place the dopped stone under the tip of the knife and in a rolling action so that the handle is raised, bring the blade tip down and cut the wax seal to the stone. As the blade never leaves the table, the risk of the knife slipping is reduced to a minimum.

The alternative method is to place the dopped stone in the freezing compartment of the refrigerator for about three minutes. The seal will then break easily by hand.

Having redopped the stone, domed side up, the next step is to finish grinding it on the 220 grit wheel.

A series of cuts are now placed all around the stone starting from a shade above the setting edge and finishing on the top of the stone. To cut through the setting edge will, of course, render the stone unsymmetrical. The best way to perform this operation is to start the round cuts with the dopped stone in the position shown in the illustration and as the stone is continually turned, bring the dop around towards the right.

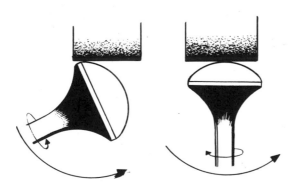

*In the final shaping the dopped stone is turned against the 220 grit wheel and at the same time stroked from left to right.*

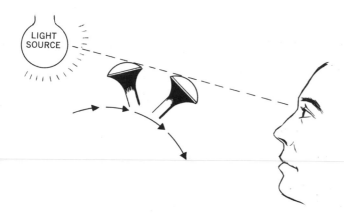

*To check the smoothness and symmetry of the cut stone, test it against a bright light in the manner shown.*

Repeat the process carefully several times, remembering that less pressure is required in this process than in the earlier rough grinding.

A smooth curve must be evident when the stone is viewed from either the front or the side although the angle of the curve from the former will, of course, be higher than the latter.

At this stage, care must also be taken to avoid a slight tendency for a stone to have a flat top. This fairly common fault is not desirable and must be put right before sanding is commenced.

When you think you have completed this stage, thoroughly examine the stone from every angle. To do this effectively, silhouette the stone at arm's length endwise, and gently turn it towards you. This will highlight any small bump. Repeat the process to check any irregularities of the side view by turning the stone in its plane through 90°.

Once a high spot has been detected it is a simple matter to remove it. To do this, it is necessary to lean forward towards the grinder, a little further than usual and roll the stone in the same way as before until the offending bump shows up.

A good strong light is recommended in all stages of cutting and polishing and at this stage an additional help can be used by placing in the tray directly in line with eye, stone and wheel, a piece of punched metal painted white. This material often is used as a back plate for house numbers and sometimes on letter boxes. A 12 in. x 5 in. piece costs about 50 cents at any hardware store and this can be cut into two, three or even four pieces as desired.

The water from the wheel washes the waste material and grit through the many small holes punched in the metal into the tray so that a clear white surface is always presented beneath the stone providing a perfect base to silhouette it for accurate cutting. The special value of this device is that it aids the cutter at a time when every care is vital to progress.

If the final work of shaping the stone on the 220 wheel is done well and thoroughly, less time will be spent at all of the subsequent stages. Fine grinding is only completed when the stone is completely symmetrical from base to crown all around.

The stone must now be sanded. Good and efficient sanding begins during the finish grinding stage. If this is done accurately, the sanding process is both easy and short. During this smoothing operation as well as the pumice and putty operations, make use of the variation of speed available depending on whether the stone is worked on the centre of the disc or on the edge of it.

The stone is worked on the face of the disc in a similar round motion to that of the 220 grinder. It also should be worked from end to end across the crown and from side to side. Keep the stone moving at all times and never let it rest in the one spot, otherwise a flat is certain to result.

Always work on that side of the wheel where the rotation is directed towards the bench, as this permits greater control over the movement of the stone by hand.

When checking the progress of the stone in the sanding, pumice or putty operations, avoid wiping the stone clean on your apron as it will inevitably become contaminated with coarser grit from earlier operations. Make it a habit to rinse the stone clean when checking or use disposable tissues.

As the cutting or smoothing rate of a new sander is faster than a used one, less pressure is required on the stone. On a worn sander, it is quite often possible to get better sanding by using the centre of the sanding disc or sometimes the last half-inch on the outside as these areas (particularly the former) often have been neglected in earlier use.

The sanding cloth must be kept damp during the process. In the past, a piece of sponge or a small paint brush with water has been used, but these methods have drawbacks, both in the amount of water thrown off and left lying on the bench, and in the risk of contamination to the sanding disc. For instance, when using two sponges, one for the 320 and the other for the 500, the wrong sponge is often picked up.

However, just over a year ago I discovered that a popular type of ladies' hair spray bottle provided an ideal way of applying the necessary moisture. These bottles, which operate by pressing a centre plunger, can be purchased for approximately 85 cents. The fine spray covers the whole face of the sanding disc and the throw-off is reduced to a minimum, while contamination is impossible.

*The beauty of beads made from natural gemstones rewards the hours of drudgery necessary to create them. The necklaces shown belong to Mrs. Elizabeth Fry, of Burwood, Vic.*

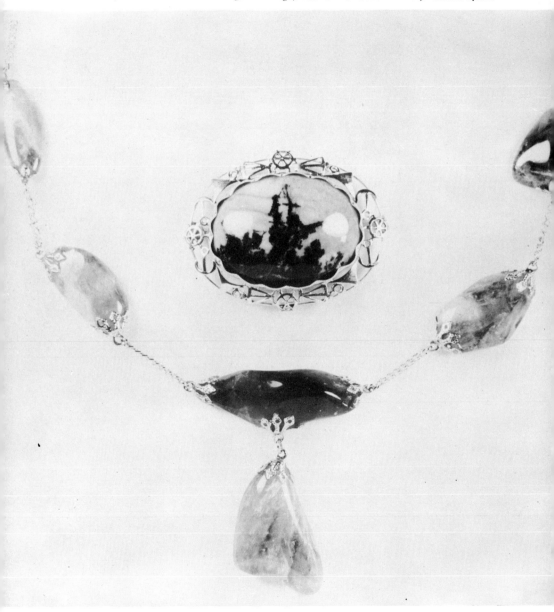

*Illustrations on this and the opposite page display the contrast between handmade and bought settings. Much credit is due to home workers who refuse to be discouraged by the elegance of factory-produced items now available.*

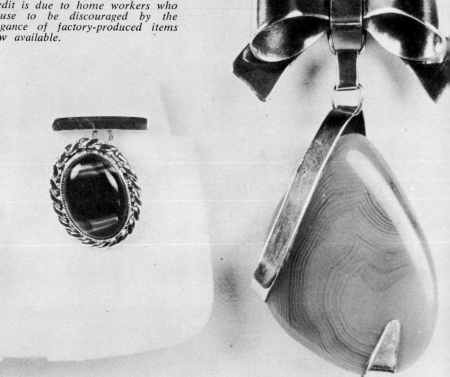

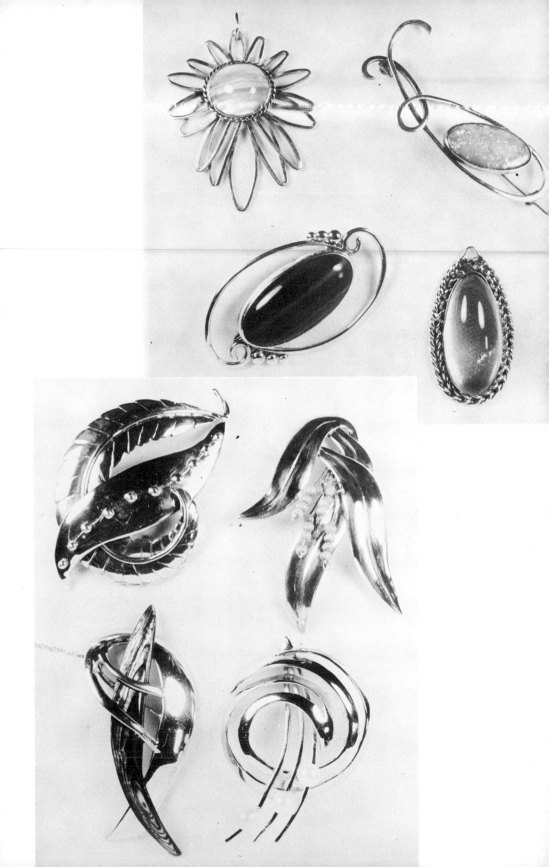

*This charming exhibit — matching silver necklet and earrings and cleverly-designed bracelet — is typical of items on display at this exhibition, where good taste and elegance of design combined with craftsmanship of a high order. Yet it was all the work of amateurs.*

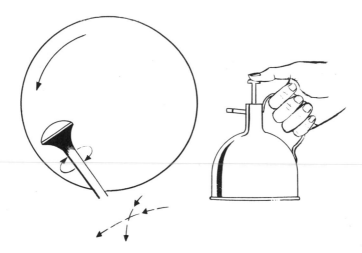

*Sanding: The stone is kept moving against the disc, being turned and also rocked as the arrows indicate. A hairspray bottle provides the best method of wetting the disc.*

From this stage onwards cleanliness is imperative. If a sander, pumice or putty wheel has one piece of foreign grit embedded in the surface, the stone being polished can have at least 350 scratches within one minute.

All wheel marks left by the 220 wheel must be completely erased before coarse sanding is complete. Then wash both hands and dopped stone.

Sanding with the 500 disc is identical to the previous process and this is not complete until all scratches left by the 320 disc are removed.

Care must be taken during the sanding stages that the stone is not allowed to become too hot. This can either cause the wax to become warm and bend or cause the stone to crack and sometimes both.

By the end of the 500 sanding, the cabochon will be showing some signs of a dull polish. Again wash hands and stone.

Neither obsidian, opalite nor goldstone has any tendency to undercut (this is a condition brought about by varying hardnesses in the stone which causes some portions of it—usually the softer areas—to remain unpolished) and therefore the pumice wheel is the next operation.

To improve the bonding of felt and pumice, the wheel should be moistened with water first and the slurry of pumice powder and water is then applied to the wheel by means of a brush (preferably one which has a plastic ferrule as brushes with tin ferrules eventually rust, so that flakes of metal fall into the slurry).

The stone is worked in a similar manner to that on the sander. As the pumice is used and thrown off, it will be necessary to recharge the wheel with more. It is the pumice powder which does the polishing, not the felt, which is merely a medium to carry the pumice.

If working conditions are clean with little risk of contamination from dust particles, the pumice thrown off and deposited in the trough may be picked up with the brush and used again.

The stone will take a fairly high polish on the pumice wheel, but the operation is not complete until all dull spots have been removed. Do not forget to finish off by washing both stone and hands.

The last stage is the putty wheel. For this a mixture of tin oxide, one to two teaspoons to a pint of water, is required. Once again moisten the wheel before the polishing mixture is applied. It is usually only necessary to wet the centre of the wheel as centrifugal force will carry the mixture to the edge.

The same type of spray bottle as we used for sanding is recommended for the putty mixture. I have used both tin oxide and cerium oxide in these sprays for over twelve months without having the plunger clogged. Should this occur, however, it is the work of a moment to dismantle, clean and reassemble.

Under *no* circumstances should the mixture which is thrown off and accumulates in the bottom of the trough be used again. Only clean mixture must be applied to the putty wheel.

Although putty powder is obtainable at most hardware stores, it is advisable to obtain the powder from a lapidary dealer as this has been triple refined and carries no impurities.

In both the pumice and putty operations, always keep the wheel wet and do not allow it to dry out during use.

The completed stone should be symmetrical from all angles and display a brilliant polish, without any trace of a scratch.

USE OF THE LEATHER WHEEL: The leather wheel is used for those stones which have an inclination to undercut such as prase, leopardskin jasper, rhodonite, and so on.

Having worked the stone on the 500 grit sander, it is good practice to carry on working the stone on a well worn 500 disc. These worn sanders are usually discarded, but it pays to keep one or two on hand for the final preparation before going to the leather wheel. It is often good policy to reduce the amount of water sprayed on when using a well worn disc as this tends to improve the polish.

The putty mixture is directed to the centre of the leather wheel and the stone worked in the same manner as on the felt discs.

SOFT CANVAS BUFF: Some stones of fibrous structure such as tiger-eye must be sanded at right angles to the compacted parallel layers of the fibres. This reduces the tendency for fibres to pull out. Pumice and subsequent polishing should be done in the same way.

However, some stones will not take a perfect polish on either felt or leather and the lapidary will never be satisfied with the results. Everyone has experienced this at some time or another and the following is a description of a soft canvas buff which can easily be made, and produces outstanding results on some of these difficult stones.

An 8 in. wooden disc is turned with a dome of approximately ¾ in. at the centre tapering to ³⁄₁₆ in. at the edge, and is then painted with a clear lacquer and allowed to dry. The lacquer will prevent possible warping due to water.

Over this dome, place a layer of clear plastic sheeting which is thumb tacked to the back of the disc. A layer of compressed crumbed sponge plastic of 1 in. thick is then cut in an 8 in. circle and placed on top of the clear plastic.

A piece of 10 oz. canvas is then placed over the crumbed plastic, pulled down and fastened by thumb tacks at the back of the disc. Folds in the canvas at the edge of the wheel should be such that with the subsequent direction of travel of the wheel, the stone will ride over, rather than dig in, during the polishing process.

Use cerium oxide instead of putty powder on this buff, spraying on and allowing to soak in before setting in motion. The buff should be kept very wet for good results and plain water can be sprayed on occasionally to advantage. Results are not immediate and 15 minutes' work would not be unusual.

I have seen unrewarding pieces of tiger-eye, ribbonstone and azurite with malachite inclusions become showpieces on this buff. It is not a

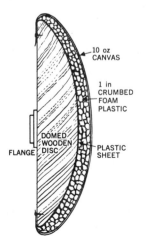

10 oz CANVAS

1 in CRUMBED FOAM PLASTIC

DOMED WOODEN DISC

FLANGE

PLASTIC SHEET

*This home-made canvas polishing buff is Lloyd Meller's tip for putting a mirror finish on the difficult stones.*

cure-all for every difficult stone, but it is certainly worth trying with any stones causing concern.

For instance, a piece of Tampa Bay (Florida) colony coral of orange and white colouring, composed basically of agate with many inclusions of calcite, had never been satisfactory in the final polish, due to under-cutting. After forty minutes on this buff it now has a mirror finish all over.

As yet, this type of soft canvas buff has never been widely tried out in Australia and very few lapidaries seem to have one. But for anyone entertaining ideas of competition, it is a must. I used one of the buffs in my home workshop for nine months, and it was so successful that I decided to place one in the local evening college.

ECONOMICAL GRINDING: The method of grinding previously described in-so-far as the angle and portion of the cutting face of the wheel on which the stone is worked are concerned, does not lend itself to economical grinding. This is due to the fact that most of the work is done in the middle of the cutting face. This very quickly results in valleys appearing in the face of the wheel despite efforts to vary the position of the stone while in use.

When a small valley appears in the wheel the usual reaction is to continue using the centre and this soon deepens the valley. As a result, very soon the wheel face has to be trimmed with a diamond dressed and on occasions, anything up to half an inch in depth has to be cut away so that the wheel will once again have a smooth face. The material removed by these wheel dressers often represents an equal amount of the wheel face to that already used. This means that only 50 per cent of the usable cutting available has been obtained from the wheel.

When a number of people are using the wheel this can represent a considerable amount of waste.

After the student has firmly implanted in his mind the necessary requirements and processes of the grinding stages and the desired final shape, he should be encouraged to make use of the grinding wheels in a totally different manner to that I have previously outlined.

Utilising the methods now described has obviated the necessity of dressing grinding wheels for the past two years at an evening college where three lapidary classes are held each week.

No doubt the method will be open to criticism, but it has not resulted in any drop in the standard of work completed, nor has it caused any inconvenience. In fact, once mastered, it can to a small degree accelerate cutting.

Good distribution of water over the whole face of the wheel is the first essential. Right from the outset the stone must be moved from side to side right across the whole wheel face whilst also being turned around in the fingers. Providing this movement is maintained a valley will never appear in the wheel.

It will be noted that grinding in this manner is done blind, as it is difficult to see the shape of the stone as it is being ground. Still, by perseverance and by acquiring a touch combined with constant checking, this problem is soon overcome.

It is also possible to partially trim a dopped stone on the 220 wheel using a similar technique.

For the doming of the stone and for most of the work in fact, the stone should be presented to the wheel in an uptilted manner to reduce any tendency to chip. A light pressure is essential at the start to grind off the right angle of the stone presented to the wheel so as to establish a working face for further shaping of the stone. Should a firm pressure be used, there is a risk of the stone digging in with the result that the upper side of it will quickly be forced down and the inscribed line cut through.

If held down the other way, although there is better water flow due to the pick-up by the stone itself, the stone will tend to bump against the wheel and could be cracked.

Should the wheel already have a valley with sharp edges it is best to work one high point at a time and then work on the other high spot until the wheel has a level face.

COMPETITION HINTS: Hobby workers who are ambitious to win prizes for their cabochons in competitions should bear in mind these points:

Usually the first step of adjudicators in competitions is to reject stones with obvious flaws, those lacking symmetry or those badly polished.

While polish and symmetry are the most important factors, in assessing the degree of polish consideration is given to whether the stone is easy to polish or not. A stone which is difficult to polish will usually be preferred to one that polishes easily.

Attention is also given to the evenness of the setting edge and, as I mentioned before, all cabochons entered in competitions must be polished on the back.

SETTINGS: Cabochons are secured in bought settings, either silver or various alloys or plated with gold or rhodium, by means of epoxy cement or in some cases by claws and by methods similar to those described in Chapter Two.

Jewellery made with cabochons is naturally more sophisticated and elaborate than that in which baroque stones are employed. It therefore offers greater opportunities for attractive design.

The use of a template corresponding to the setting for which the cabochon is intended simplifies the work without making it any less interesting. Templates cut in a variety of shapes are produced to standard sizes and offer considerable scope to the designer.

Those who despise using a template on the grounds that it is a restrictive mechanical aid will need a millimetre gauge to match their stones and settings. But this need create no problem because settings are now available for cabochons of almost any size and shape.

Illustrations elsewhere in this book demonstrate the beauty and originality which it is possible to achieve in jewellery made with bought settings.

## COSTS

Plastic templates, 75 cents to $3; brass and aluminium marking pencils, 5 cents each; spirit lamp, $1.28; dopping wax, 45 cents to 60 cents a lb.

Grinding wheels, 6 in., $2.80 to $3.35; 8 in., $4.30 to $5.30; diamond wheel truers, $5.75 to $6; sanding discs, 6 in., 45c to 50c; 8 in., 65c to 75c; rubber backing discs, 6 in., 20c to 55c; 8 in., 30c to 70c; peel-off cement, $\frac{1}{2}$-pint, 54c to $1.65.

Felt discs, 6 in., $1 to $4; 8 in., $3.60 to $7; leather buffs, 85c to $1.25.

Polishing powders, pumice, 10c a lb.; tripoli, 25c to 80c a lb.; tin oxide, $2.50 to $2.80 a lb.; cerium oxide, $1.25 a $\frac{1}{4}$ lb.; Linde A, $2 to $2.50 an oz.

These prices were quoted at the end of 1966, and are subject to fluctuation. They are not binding on any lapidary supply house.

# MAKING A GEMSTONE NECKLACE

Polished gemstones make a most attractive necklace, although shaping the individual beads involves many hours of dull and repetitive work on the 100 and 220 grit wheels.

Selected materials should not be too heavy for comfortable wear. Specific gravity offers a guide to weight and the range of lighter gemstones is wide, including agate, bowenite, chert and sodalite as well as all the quartz varieties.

Mr. Fred Sewell, of Bathurst Lapidary Club, some of whose work is illustrated, preforms his beads from slabs cut to size. After rough shaping on the coarse wheel, Mr. Sewell does all the fine grinding and polishing in his tumbling machine.

When tumbling beads, containers should be plastic or rubber-lined as a precaution against damage and buffer material added in a ratio of one part to every four of the load.

*Beads call for many hours of patient work. These necklaces were made by Mr Fred Sewell of the Bathurst Lapidary Club. On the left is a necklace of yellow carnelian agate from Bellata, NSW and on the right one of petrified wood cut into elongated octagon shapes. All the beads were preformed and tumbled, then strung together with U-pegs and jump rings.*

Hand-drilling beads in the bench vice is a very tedious task indeed, but care is necessary when using a power drill to see that the hole passes through the centre or thickest part of the bead. Some sort of clamp will be needed with every shape of bead but a conical jig having a hole at the apex offers a good means of holding round beads.

Solid drills charged with diamond dust or silicon carbide grits can be used to make small holes. But Mr. Sewell has found an easier way than stringing his beads. He joins them most effectively with U-pegs and jump rings.

Oblong or oval cabochon beads are easier to shape than spheres. Material for round beads must be sawn into cubes and then have the corners removed on the 100 grit wheel. Perfect spheres are then produced by grinding with a couple of pieces of iron or brass pipe of appropriate diameter.

One pipe should be secured to the chuck of a lathe or the arbor of a grinder so that it can be spun. The other piece should be long enough for handling. The working ends of both pipes are bevelled and plugged with cotton waste soaked in a mixture of 220 grit and water. The rough spheres are taken in turn between the two pipes, being manipulated by the one held in the bead-cutter's hand. More grit is applied as the sphere is ground to shape.

A graduated necklace of round beads calls for pipe ends of various sizes. Bear in mind that the resulting sphere will be a third larger than the diameter of the pipe used.

# 5

# RAINBOWS OF FIRE

A RAY OF LIGHT falls on a diamond and a star is born. The stone, itself colourless and transparent as a block of ice, is transformed to a fragment of living fire. It sparkles, glitters, flashes in vivid, vibrating colours—orange-red, yellow and green-blue.

The colours do not come from the diamond but from the light itself. They have been created in the same way that raindrops create the colours of the rainbow. This process is known technically as dispersion and the dispersion of two man-made gemstones, titania and fabulite, is so great that they display miniature rainbows.

Like raindrops, these transparent crystals split light into the colours of the spectrum, which range from red to violet by way of yellow, green and blue. This effect is due to the varying speeds at which different colours of light travel. It is seen whenever light emerges from a refractive medium, such as glass or water, in which the surfaces are not parallel to each other.

Refraction is the term used to describe the bending of light rays which occurs as the light passes through materials of different optical density.

*Reflection, refraction, dispersion—the ways in which light behaves within a properly-proportioned brilliant gemstone.*

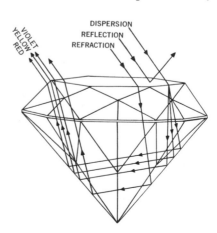

The extent of this bending is shown as an index of refraction, which is a figure giving the ratio of the speed of light in air to its speed in the substance concerned. The difference between the refractive indices of red and violet light rays provides a scale by which to measure dispersion.

Natural crystal shapes in which gemstones occur, of which there are seven basic systems—isometric (cubic), tetragonal, orthorhombic, monoclinic, triclinic, hexagonal and rhombohedral or trigonal—also have a part in gem optics. Most crystal systems except the isometric cause light rays to split into two. This is known as double refraction and it sometimes leads to the stone showing two different colours. This is called dichroism. Gems possessing more than two colours are described as being pleochroic.

Most gemstones are too small and their double refraction too weak to be noticed. But some stones, such as titania and the transparent variety of calcite called Iceland spar, are so strongly doubly refractive that they must be cut from the best angle of the crystal to reduce the confusion of lights produced when the stone is faceted.

Refraction and reflection are properties which the gem-cutter must be able to exploit to the full if he is to make the best of waterwhite and light-coloured gems. The refractive indices of these stones are a reliable guide to their potential brilliance.

The index of refraction, as a measure of the optical density of the stone, also indicates how much light will be reflected from it. Gems with high refractive indices, such as diamonds and zircons, will reflect light from steeper angles than those with lower refractive indices.

It is this fact which explains the effectiveness of the brilliant cut. This style is supposed to have been devised by a Venetian diamond-cutter named Vincenzio Peruggi about 300 years ago. The standard brilliant has 57 facets—the flat surfaces cut to reflect light—including the upper surface of the stone, which is called the table.

This is one of the names for the parts of a gemstone which have come down to us from history. The earliest faceted forms were known as table cuts. The bevelled edge of this style, being the widest part of the stone, became known as the girdle. That part of the stone above the girdle is called the crown while the part below is the pavilion, which is also known as the back of the stone.

The brilliant cut has 32 facets on the crown, excluding the table, and 24 pavilion facets. On the crown are eight star facets at the table edge, eight main facets between table and girdle and 16 girdle facets. There are eight main and 16 girdle facets on the pavilion.

The index of refraction not only acts as a guide to the main facet angles of a brilliant cut stone, but as a consequence the proportions of the

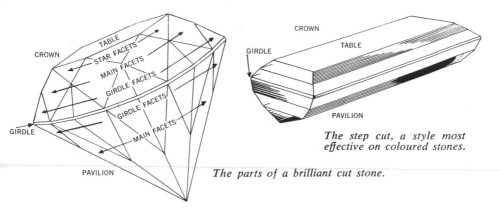

*The step cut, a style most effective on coloured stones.*

*The parts of a brilliant cut stone.*

gem as well. This means that the greatest depth or thickness of the stone should be between three-fifths or four-fifths the greatest breadth or spread. The diameter of the table varies from two-fifths to three-fifths that of the girdle.

These proportions only apply to waterwhite or light-coloured gems. The table would be smaller for a dark-hued stone, the crown facet angles less steep and the depth of the pavilion increased in relation to the crown.

Coloured gems are often cut in the second basic style of faceted stones —the step cut. This style is so much favoured for one particular gem that a variant of it is known as the emerald cut. Here again the index of refraction serves as a guide to the best angles for the main facets. In the case of the step cut these are the facets at the apex of the pavilion and the middle of the crown.

The table of the step cut stone should be from two-fifths to three-fifths the width of the girdle at its narrowest side. The girdle width should also be between twice and one-and-a-half times the depth of the pavilion, with between two and four crown facets and three or more pavilion facets according to size.

At this stage it should be emphasised that faceting is an art, not a science. Although it is easy to produce a gem of ideal proportions by mathematics on paper, cutting the same stone from the rough is likely to be complicated by flaws, either in the texture or the colour. This may mean that both faceting angles and proportions have to be adjusted but there is no harm in that providing the changes are not drastic and the general shape of the stone remains the same. Figures given for facet angles can be altered by up to five degrees in most instances without spoiling the eventual stone.

It is the same with faceting techniques. Cutting and polishing faceted stones is carried out on a variety of horizontal laps, mostly of metal but sometimes of wood, plastic or waxed calico. Every gem-cutter has his own ideas about the right type of lap and polishing agent to use for each variety of gem.

In practice the learner will find that he can obtain satisfactory results with almost any stone using copper laps charged with cutting and polishing grades of diamond dust. However there is no doubt that special treatments evolved over the years help to achieve perfection with certain stones. For that reason, they are included in the following list:

## ALEXANDRITE

This variety of the otherwise yellow-green gemstone chrysoberyl is dark green or blue-green in daylight and raspberry red by artificial light owing to the delicate colour balance of the chromium it contains. It was first discovered in 1833 in the emerald mines of Russia's Ural Mountains. The day had been already marked for celebration of the coming-of-age of the future Tsar Alexander II and the new gemstone was named after him. Red and green were the colours of the Imperial Guard and this confirmed the popularity of alexandrite in Tsarist Russia.

It is still prized for its rarity and quality. Varying from transparent to translucent, alexandrite is hardness $8\frac{1}{2}$ on Mohs' scale. Its refractive index is 1.74 to 1.75 and colour dispersion 0.015. The main facet angles are 40 degrees for both crown and pavilion and a well proportioned stone will have a table whose diameter is three-fifths that of the girdle. Polish on a tin lap with tripoli or 0-2 micron diamond dust. Diamond dust on a boxwood lap gives an excellent finish.

The best alexandrite comes from Siberia and Ceylon. Gem chrysoberyl is more common, occurring also in the United States, Ireland and Brazil. In Brazil and Ceylon, it is also found as greenish, silky cat's-eye cymophane, which shows a moving line of light when cut as a cabochon. Specific gravity varies from 3.50 to 3.84.

## APATITE

Gem quality varieties of this phosphate mineral are blue-green nioroxite and yellow-green asparagus stone. Usually green, apatite may also occur red, yellow, blue or colourless. Translucent to opaque. Hardness $4\frac{1}{2}$ to 5. Refractive index 1.63 to 1.65 and colour dispersion 0.013. The main facet angles are 40 degrees for the crown and 32 degrees for the pavilion. Apatite is not an easy stone to cut, being brittle as well as soft. It is very likely to crack if overheated either when dopping or polishing. Polish on a tin or boxwood lap with a wet mixture of tin oxide, but a cautious final whirl on an almost dry lap is needed to develop a brilliant finish. Faceting stone is imported to Australia from Mexico. S.G. from 3.15 to 3.23.

## AQUAMARINE

The most common gem variety of the mineral beryl, transparent and usually blue to sea-green in colour. The colour of some stones is improved by heating. Hardness according to Mohs' scale is 7½ to 8, refractive index 1.57-1.58, and colour dispersion 0.014. The main facet angles are 42 degrees for the crown and 43 degrees for the pavilion. The diameter of the table should be half that of the girdle.

The most valuable of all gemstones, the emerald, is related to the aquamarine. The velvety green colour that makes all the difference is due

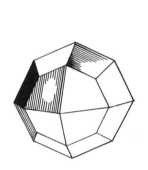

*Garnet (left) and beryl crystals.*                    *Cassiterite crystal.*

to the merest trace of the metallic element chromium. Transparent stones of both clear and golden beryl also make nice gems. A variety of yellow beryl found in South-West Africa is called heliodor and pink to rose-red beryl is morganite.

All the beryl gems are polished on a tin lap using tin oxide and all have a fine texture that polishes easily. Emerald, however, is very brittle. It cracks easily and is subject to flaws which may become unsightly through picking up dirt and polish. This problem also affects aquamarine to a lesser degree. Concentration and a light touch on the lap are essential.

Gem quality beryls are found in Queensland, New England, South Australia and Western Australia, emeralds being mined at Emmaville, N.S.W., and a number of places in Western Australia. Colombia, South

America, leads the world in producing emeralds, with India, Russia, Brazil and the United States as main sources of most of the beryl gems. Morganite comes from Madagascar. S.G. from 2.63 to 2.87.

## CASSITERITE

Brown and black crystals of this tin ore are sometimes faceted on the crown to display their remarkable glitter and fire—their colour dispersion rating 00.71 far exceeds the 0.044 of the diamond. Main facet angles of around 40 degrees will be suitable.

Cassiterite is not easy to polish, but Linde A powder on a tin lap should give good results if the lap is cut to its slowest speed and is kept almost dry in its final stages.

The mineral occurs throughout Australia but has been extensively mined. Gem quality crystals occur in the New England district of New South Wales. Hardness is 6½ on Mohs' scale. S.G. from 6.8 to 7.1.

## EPIDOTE

This complex silicate mineral so often occurs in a pistachio shade of green that one of its lesser-known names is pistacite. It is not as often cut as it deserves to be in Australia, although gem quality crystals have been picked up around Olary, South Australia. Varieties found overseas can also be reddish, when the mineral is called piedmontite, or brown to black as allanite. Light-coloured epidote with a low iron content is known as clinozoisite.

It is hardness 6½ on Mohs' scale and polishes well with Linde A on a tin lap. Caution must be exercised in cutting because the crystals possess perfect cleavage and split easily. Main facet angles are 40 degrees on both crown and pavilion. Dark stones look better as cabochons.

Sources of high quality material include the Austrian Tyrol, France, Italy and Norway in Europe, and various localities in the United States and Brazil.

## FIRE OPAL

This is almost transparent opal coloured in vivid reds and orange-reds, typically Mexican in origin, although stones of this type are also found in Australia. Water opal, which shows a play of colour like drops of iridescent water, also provides material for faceting. Transparent opal which has neither vivid colour nor iridescence, is known as hyalite.

The hardness of opal varies from 5 to 6½ on Mohs' scale and the index of refraction is 1.44 to 1.45. Angles for main facets are 45 degrees for the crown and 43 degrees for the pavilion. A well-proportioned stone will have a table that is half the width of the girdle. Polish with tin oxide on a boxwood or pewter lap. As opal is very heat-shy and tends to craze, use plenty of water and apply the polishing agent as a thin creamy mixture.

## FLUORITE

This is the odd, one—a widely distributed mineral that occurs in beautiful crystals of green, yellow, blue-green and purple, some of which glow bright blue under ultra-violet light, giving the name to fluorescence. These attractive stones would be favourites for jewellery but for their softness—only hardness 4 on Mohs' scale—brittleness and perfect cleavage in four directions.

Fluorite rewards all the trouble it takes to facet although it can be worn only occasionally. It is transparent to translucent, the index of refraction is 1.43 and the colour dispersion 0.007. Angles for the main facets are 45 degrees on the crown and 43 degrees on the pavilion. Tin oxide on a wax lap produces a good polish but fluorite is so heat-shy that dopping and cutting must be done most cautiously.

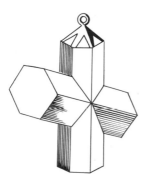

*Twinned crystals of staurolite are known as fairy cross stone and often have a bell-cap mounted on one end.*

*Matched natural crystals of fluorite make attractive earrings mounted on bought findings.*

A friend of mine has a charming matched set of jewellery made from seven natural translucent blue-green fluorite crystals in the familiar cubic double pyramid shape. Two of these crystals are mounted as drop earrings on bought sterling silver findings while the other five form a necklet suspended from a silver chain.

Australia produces gem quality fluorite, but the United States is the world's leading producer and the Blue John of English mines is also famous. Most unusual is the banded material from Mexico some of which displays four colours. An alternative name for the mineral is fluorspar. S.G. from 3 to 3.2.

## GARNET

A few members of this large mineral family occur as transparent to translucent gem quality stones. The most spectacular of these is the brilliant green variety called demantoid, often sold as an emerald but far brighter than that stone. Demantoid garnet has the unusually high dispersion factor of 0.057, greater than that of a diamond and remarkable for a coloured stone. Another green garnet, the darker hessonite, is rated 0.027 like the hyacinth-red spessartite and the darker red almandite. Both almandite and the ruby-red pyrope, which has a dispersion of 0.022, are known as precious garnet.

Garnets vary from the hardness $6\frac{1}{2}$ of demantoid on Mohs' scale to the $7\frac{1}{2}$ of almandite. S.G. from 3.5 to 4.3. The indices of refraction range from 1.75 of pyrope and hessonite to 1.89 of demantoid. Main facet angles of all varieties are 40 degrees on both crown and pavilion.

Polish on a tin lap with Linde A powder. Often garnets contain flaws such as feathering, cracks and inclusions. Cavities are often disclosed in both hessonite and almandite crystals during cutting. The likelihood of these faults is the main complication when faceting garnets, providing care is taken to prevent overheating which might crack some stones. Polishing the softer demantoid is best carried out with a slow-running lap that is almost dry.

Gem quality almandite, pyrope and hessonite garnets have come from New England, pyropes from Lowood, Queensland, almandite and spessartite from Broken Hill, N.S.W., and almandite from the eastern Macdonnell Ranges. Top world sources of pyrope, almandite, demantoid and hessonite garnets respectively are the Transvaal province of South Africa, India, Russia's Ural Mountains and Ceylon. Garnets of several varieties are found at Colorado and other places in the United States, West Germany and Brazil.

## HEMATITE

In gem quality this important iron ore consists of lustrous, metallic steel-grey to black crystals and hematite of this kind forms only a fraction of the world's supplies. Both faceted and cut as cabochons, it is often used for men's jewellery. Its hardness—$5\frac{1}{2}$ to $6\frac{1}{2}$ on Mohs' scale—has made hematite the classic medium for intaglio (sunken) carving over hundreds of years.

Faceting is usually confined to the crown as the material is opaque. Main facets of 45 degrees will do very well. When carefully polished on a tin lap with Linde A powder, hematite lives up to its nickname of black diamond. A slow lap that is almost dry puts a final high polish on the stone.

Gem quality hematite occurs on the Island of Elba, Norway, Sweden, several localities in the United States, England, and at St. Gothard, Switzerland where the attractive groups of crystals known as iron roses are found. S.G. from 4.95 to 5.16.

## IOLITE

This three-colour gemstone is blue, brown or yellow according to the way in which the light strikes it. Therefore the crystal must be oriented so that it can be cut to show the best colour, usually the clear blue.

Iolite is hardness 7 to $7\frac{1}{2}$ on Mohs' scale. Colour dispersion 0.017. Main facet angles are 45 degrees for the crown and 43 degrees for the pavilion. Although it has only a vitreous lustre, the stone polishes well with tin oxide on a tin lap.

## JET

Compact black variety of lignite coal, too soft—hardness $2\frac{1}{2}$ to 4 on Mohs' scale—to work with power tools. It is best cut and polished by hand, using a penknife, file and strips of silicon carbide paper folded on a narrow strip of board. Facet angles and styles do not matter much although crown mains about 40 degrees should be right. Tin oxide on a piece of chamois should produce a brilliant finish. Jet, a much-neglected material nowadays, also makes attractive cabochons and is specially suitable for the semi-faceted forms known as pendeloque (as earrings) and winged cabochons.

The world's finest jet comes from a 20 ft. seam at Whitby, England, and this is now quite scarce. Other sources are in Spain, France and various localities in the United States. S.G. from 1.20 to 1.30.

## KUNZITE

This delicate lilac-pink variety of the mineral spodumene fluoresces brilliant orange-pink when exposed to X-rays or ultraviolet light and continues to phosphoresce for a short time afterwards. It is hardness 7 on Mohs' scale and its indices of refraction are 1.66 to 1.67. Colour dispersion 0.017. Both the main crown and pavilion facets are cut at an angle of 40 degrees and the diameter of the table should be about three-fifths that of the girdle. Polish with tin oxide on a tin lap but the easy cleavage calls for cutting the table about 70 degrees off the grain.

The colour of kunzite gems often fades when exposed to strong sunlight. First found in 1903, it was named for the distinguished U.S. gemmologist Dr. George Frederick Kunz. A related gem variety of spodumene is the transparent yellow-green to emerald-green hiddenite. Main sources of both gems are in the United States—hiddenite in North Carolina and kunzite in California. Kunzite is also found in Brazil and Madagascar. S.G. 3.2.

## KYANITE

A unique feature of kyanite is its variable hardness, the long-bladed crystals rating only 4½ on Mohs' scale along their length but 6-7 across their width. A knife will scratch kyanite in one direction but not in the other and this poses obvious problems for the gem-cutter. As a result the stone is most often seen as a cabochon. It can be faceted, however, providing both grinding and polishing are carried out with a gentle touch and always with the grain.

Although the name of this gem comes from a Greek word meaning blue, it is usually colourless, white or grey with blue streaks. A beautiful pale green variety is found in North Carolina, U.S.A. Colour dispersion 0.020. The refractive indices are 1.71 to 1.73 so that the main facet angles for the crown are 37 degrees and for the pavilion 42 degrees. Polish with Linde A on a tin lap.

The finest crystals are found near St. Gothard, Switzerland. Other sources are in India, Brazil and the Kola Peninsula, U.S.S.R. S.G. from 3.56 to 3.67.

## OBSIDIAN

This natural volcanic glass is usually black, but sometimes red, mottled black and red, brown, grey or banded with combinations of these colours. The most flamboyant obsidians are those showing golden or silvery iridescence. Stones vary from translucent to opaque, but are mostly darkened by masses of tiny beaded or rod-like inclusions known as crystallites.

Hardness is 5 to 5½ on Mohs' scale and the index of refraction is 1.50. Cutting the crown mains at 45 degrees and the pavilion at 43 with the diameter of the table half that of the girdle makes a nice stone, but most obsidian is too dense for facet angles to matter overmuch. Well-watered tin oxide on a boxwood or pewter lap secures a good polish.

## PERIDOT

Pale, yellowish-green gem variety of the mineral chrysolite, transparent to translucent and hardness 6½ to 7 on Mohs' scale. Its indices of refraction are 1.64 to 1.69 giving main faceting angles of 40 degrees for both crown and pavilion. Colour dispersion 0.020.

Linde A on a tin lap is the recommended polish, but peridots often have soft spots which tend to undercut instead of polishing. Slowing the lap and allowing the polish to dry out may solve the problem. Professionals use sulphuric acid in the polishing mixture but this method is not recommended to amateurs.

In the New Mexico and Arizona deserts of the United States peridots are found as pebbles known as Job's tears, but the main world source is tiny St. John Island in the Red Sea. Olive-green or brown olivines are a related gem variety of chrysolite, which are found also in Brazil and Egypt. S.G. from 3.27 to 3.42.

## PHENACITE

Usually colourless and transparent mineral not unlike rock crystal for which it is often mistaken, sometimes tinted yellow or wine-red. Phenacite is hardness 7½ to 8 on Mohs' scale and its refractive indices are 1.65 to 1.67. Colour dispersion 0.015. Main faceting angles are 40 degrees on both crown and pavilion and the table diameter should be about 55 per cent the girdle diameter. The stone polishes brilliantly but slowly with tin oxide on a tin lap, while 20-40 micron diamond dust followed by 0.2 micron on the other side of the lap would get quicker results.

Gem quality material is obtained from Brazil and various parts of the United States. It also occurs in Russia. S.G. 2.96-3.00.

## PREHNITE

Transparent specimens of this colourless, grey, yellow-green, golden-brown mineral make fine faceted gems. Prehnite is hardness 6-6½ and the refractive indices are 1.61 to 1.65. Main facet angles for the crown are 40 degrees and for the pavilion 43 degrees. Polish on a tin lap with Linde A and cut carefully as some material has a tendency to split.

## QUARTZ

No finer faceting material exists for the learner than the transparent crystalline varieties of quartz—waterwhite rock crystal, purple to bluish-violet amethyst, pink-tinted rose quartz, yellow citrines and smoky quartz or cairngorm stone, which is tawny yellow to brown-black.

Quartz is hardness 7 on Mohs' scale and the refractive indices are

1.54 to 1.57. Colour dispersion rates 0.013. Main facet angles are about 45 degrees for the crown and 43 degrees for the pavilion. Polish with tin oxide on a tin or lucite lap.

For a bright finish on all the coloured varieties of transparent quartz, give the stone a final whirl with the lap at a slow speed and the polish no more than damp to get rid of the last scratches. Amethysts appear to show the most feathering and flaws of all the quartz gems and are often streaked so that it is necessary to turn the stone to enclose the best colour in the pavilion facets.

The many beautiful transparent varieties of sagenitic quartz which enclose slender reddish-brown crystals of rutile, leek-green actinolite, chatoyant fibres of asbestos or black schorl crystals, make interesting gems if the inclusions are all sited in the pavilion of the stone and a generous layer of clear crystal left on the crown. Soaking the stone beforehand in a heated waterglass solution as advised in Chapter Two is a wise precaution.

## RHODONITE

Rose-red gem quality of this manganese silicate sometimes includes transparent material that can be faceted. Hardness is 5-6 on Mohs' scale and the index of refraction 1.66, giving main facet angles of 40 degrees for the crown and 43 degrees for the pavilion. The diameter of the table is three-fifths that of the girdle for a well-shaped stone. Polish on a tin lap with tin oxide. It will be helpful to cut down the lap speed and finish with drying powder.

## SAPPHIRE

Australia is a world source for sapphire, particularly the famous gemfield at Anakie in central Queensland where stones of all colours, including pigeon-blood red rubies have been found. Rubies have been found at other places in Queensland, South Australia, Victoria, Tasmania, and the Cudgegong River, N.S.W., but few worthwhile gemstones are reported.

*Hairlike crystals of rutile and other inclusions in sagenitic quartz should be cut into the pavilion of the stone with a layer of clear crystal above them.*

Many fine blue, yellow, green, waterwhite and parti-coloured sapphires have come from Australian fields, however, mainly Anakie and localities in the New England district of New South Wales. Some of these were extremely valuable stones. Five huge gems from Anakie, three blues and two black star sapphires, have been valued at a total of $A1,340,000. Another fine stone was the $A12,050 Golden Queen of 1952. This stone was of the deep golden hue which is typical of these Australian sapphires, which are the finest in the world.

Sapphires are hardness 9 on Mohs' scale and consequently best cut on a copper lap charged with diamond dust. The indices of refraction are 1.76 to 1.77, which give main facet angles of 37 degrees on the crown and 42 degrees on the pavilion. But facet angles are only important for the light-coloured transparent stones, facets on the darker sapphires being cut less steeply so as to give a shallower stone.

Polish on a copper or bronze lap with tripoli or on a tin or lead lap with 0.2 micron diamond dust. For a perfect finish many facets may require polishing from different directions, particularly the table. Flaws, holes and inclusions add to the risk of spoiling the gem during cutting or polishing. Colour dispersion 0.018.

The finest sapphires come from Kashmir in north-west India and are known as Kashmir blues, their colour being regarded as a paragon for gems from other places. Stones other than blue are sometimes mis-called Oriental topaz, Oriental emerald and so on. Other important sources are Burma, Ceylon, Afghanistan and Montana in the United States. S.G. from 3.90 to 4.14.

## SPHENE

Bright green or yellow gem variety of the dark brown to black mineral titanite almost as fiery as the demantoid garnet. The name sphene is the Greek word for wedge, an allusion to the shape of titanite crystals, which look rather like envelopes. Colour dispersion is 0.051, greater than the diamond, which sphenes match in lustre. The indices of refraction are 1.92 to 2.05 giving main facet angles of 43 degrees for the crown and 40 for the pavilion. In a properly proportioned gem the diameter of the table should be about three-fifths that of the girdle.

Softness—it is 5-5½ on Mohs' scale—is the drawback of this most attractive stone. Polish with tin oxide on a tin lap and finish off with a drying lap at a reduced speed.

Gem quality sphene occurs in crystal fragments on Huonville Station, 11 miles south-east of Broken Hill, N.S.W. World sources include Switzerland, Austria and several places in the United States.

## SPINEL

This gem goes right round the spectrum from the yellow to orange-red rubicelle and rose-red balas ruby to grass-green chlorospinel, blue sapphirine, violet-purple almandine, and the darker pleonaste, gahnite, picotite and hercynite, most of which merge from green shades to black. These stones also range from transparent to almost opaque with a vitreous lustre.

Spinel is hardness 8 on Mohs' scale with a refractive index of 1.72 and colour dispersion of 0.020. Main facet angles are 40 for both crown and pavilion. Polish on a tin lap with Linde A. Despite its hardness, the crystal structure of spinel sometimes makes it difficult to polish. The direction of polishing then has to be changed as well as cutting down the lap speed and using polish that is almost dry.

World sources for spinel are Ceylon, Burma, Thailand, India and Madagascar. S.G. from 3.5 to 4.

## STAUROLITE

This transparent to opaque yellowish-brown mineral is also known as fairy-stone or cross-stone from the cross-shaped twinned crystals in which it is often found. These crystals are mostly kept as specimens and sometimes made into a pendant by one of the ends being cemented to a bell-cap and hung on a chain.

Other transparent or translucent material might be faceted. Staurolite is hardness 7 to 7½ on Mohs' scale and the refractive indices are 1.63-1.65 for the red stone and 1.73-1.74 for the brown. Although the lustre is only resinous, colour dispersion rates 0.023. Main crown and pavilion facet angles should be both 40 degrees. Polish with Linde A on a tin lap.

Most Australian staurolite appears to be Queensland material. A famous source is at Monte Campione, Switzerland and the gem also occurs in Brazil and parts of the United States. S.G. from 3.6 to 3.7.

## SYNTHETICS

Most of the faceting material on sale to Australian hobby gemworkers is synthetic sapphire, ruby and spinel. Other synthetics available include alexandrite and kunzite. Synthetic purple sapphire is often sold in place of natural amethyst.

Synthetic stones respond to the same cutting and polishing techniques as their natural counterparts, except that mostly they are much less difficult than the real thing. Chemically speaking, of course, they are the real thing. On the other hand, there is a whole world of difference between a gem created in a workshop a few days ago and one that has survived several hundred million years of evolution.

Most difficult to polish are the darker varieties of synthetic spinel put out as synthetic tourmaline. Spinel is also manufactured in Australia to imitate zircon, topaz and aquamarine. Other Australian synthetics are rubies, sapphires and emeralds. Quartz is also synthesized to provide flawless crystals for the radio and electrical industry.

Imitation gems known as paste—a glass made with fused silica, potash, lead and half-a-dozen other chemicals—have been known since the 17th century. Faceted glass gems made into little mirrors by means of mercury or tin foil on the back facets are known as rhinestones.

Modern synthetics were first made by Auguste Victor Verneuil, a French chemist, 65 years ago. By exposing powdered aluminium oxide and colouring material to the flame of an oxy-hydrogen blowtorch Verneuil built up a pear-shaped ruby crystal which he called a boule. Later he experimented by adding magnesium and found he had created spinel. Many years went by before blue sapphire was correctly synthesized.

In 1935 an American chemist, Carroll F. Chatham discovered a way to grow emerald crystals in superheated solutions that were finer and more perfect than the natural gemstone.

In August, 1966, scientists of the Commonwealth Scientific Industrial Research Organisation announced that they had produced synthetic opals by a new technique. The announcement added that the synthetic opal lacked many of the characteristic features of the natural stone but showed a similar play of colours.

Scientists overseas have outdone nature by producing two completely new gemstones—titania and fabulite. Both have phenomenal colour dispersion—that of titania being 0.28 and that of fabulite. 0.19.

Titania is titanium oxide or purified synthetic rutile. It is a transparent, faintly yellow crystal quite unlike the opaque, red-brown rutile of nature. It is so strongly doubly refractive to light rays that the gem-cutter must take special measures to prevent the gem appearing blurred.

Fabulite, on the other hand, is singly refractive with an index of 2.409 compared to the 2.41-2.42 of the diamond. Chemically, it is strontium titanate, transparent, waterwhite and surpassing the diamond in almost everything except hardness—it is only $6-6\frac{1}{2}$ on Mohs' scale. Both titania and fabulite polish with Linde A on a tin lap.

## TEKTITE

This glassy greenish to brownish stone looks like a fragment of discarded beer bottle and has many names—buttonstone, australite and Darwin glass are three in use in Australia as well as tektite, which means melted rock.

What makes tektites so special is that they originated from space, either as the tail of a comet or in splashes from the surface of the moon around 10 million years ago. Their rounded shapes suggest that the tektites solidified while whirling through the air.

Hardness 5½ on Mohs' scale, tektites have refractive indices of 1.49-1.53. Main facet angles are 45 degrees for the crown and 43 degrees for the pavilion. Polish with tin oxide on a lucite lap and use the polish sparingly with plenty of water.

Tektites are widespread south of a diagonal line from the Kimberleys to Kyogle, N.S.W., including north-west Tasmania. They were first found along the Moldau River, Czechoslovakia, and also occur on some Indonesian islands and in Texas, where they are black. S.G. from 2.3 to 2.5.

## TOPAZ

This is another beautiful gem that spans the rainbow in the colours of its varieties although genuine red topaz, miscalled Brazilian ruby, is very rare. Most pink topaz has been changed from yellow by heating and the stone is known as burnt topaz in consequence.

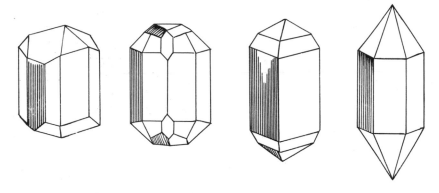

*Tourmaline (left) and topaz crystals.*      *Zircon (left) and quartz crystals.*

The colour sequence runs from the resplendent waterwhites, sometimes called Slaves' Diamonds, to yellow, orange, sherry, pale-green, blue and violet, which is another rare stone. All make delightful faceted stones, especially the blues, clear orange-yellows and waterwhites, which look as good as diamonds—and often have been passed off as them—in fancy cuts. Both yellow and blue topaz may fade on long exposure to light.

Hardness is 8 on Mohs' scale and indices of refraction range from 1.60 to 1.64 but colour dispersion is relatively small at 0.014. Main facet angles are 40 degrees for the crown and 43 degrees for the pavilion. Polishing, either with Linde A or 0-2 micron diamond dust on a tin lap, is made easier if the stone has been previously cut with the table facet a few degrees off the cleavage plane. Cleavage surfaces are notoriously hard to polish although the slower lap and almost dry polish will ultimately succeed.

Good topaz has been obtained in all States of Australia, mostly in blues and greens and especially in the New England district of New South Wales, Queensland and Beechworth, Victoria. Large crystals are found also on Flinders Island in the Bass Strait.

The gem occurs all over the world with the fabulous Minas Gerais gemfields of Brazil as the main source. The finest waterwhites come from Ceylon and blues from Madagascar. Various localities in Russia, Britain and the United States also produce fine topaz. S.G. from 3.53 to 3.58.

## TOURMALINE

Scientifically, this is perhaps the most fascinating of all the gemstones. Experts agree to disagree on the precise details of its complex chemical composition—$(Na, Ca) (Li, Mg, Fe, Al)_9 B_3 Si_6 (O, OH)_{31}$—while utilising the remarkable polarising action on light, dichroism and peculiar electrical properties of its crystals. The last-named enable tourmalines to be used as depth gauges in submarines.

Their chemistry divides tourmalines into three groups—those containing iron, mostly black; those with magnesia, mostly brown, and the alkili tourmalines, the group which shows all the rich colours—pink or red rubellite, rich green, deep blue indicolite and waterwhite achroite. Two or more of these colours are seen in many crystals either as bands or stripes, often combinations of red, green, waterwhite and black. These combinations are varied so that no two crystals appear alike.

Hardness is 7-7½ on Mohs' scale and the indices of refraction vary from 1.60 to 1.65 over the variously coloured stones. Colour dispersion is 0.017. Main facet angles are 40 degrees on both crown and pavilion, with the diameter of the table three-fifths that of the girdle.

Polish on a tin lap with Linde A although the darker stones require a slower lap and powder only slightly damp. Polishing from another direction may be needed to remove all the scratches. Flaws and feathering disfigure many crystals and overheating should be avoided. Owing to polarisation, table facets must be cut almost parallel to the crystal face.

Tourmalines most often found in Australia are schorl, the black variety, although fine coloured stones have been mined in South Australia, mainly at Daws Diggings and near Penneshaw on Kangaroo Island. Main overseas sources are Madagascar, south-west Africa, the Italian island of Elba, India, Ceylon, Burma, Russia, Brazil and parts of the United States. S.G. from 2.9 to 3.1.

## ZIRCON

Transparent zircons in a rich variety of colour have a dispersive power of 0.039, almost as bright as a diamond. However, many of these gems owe their colour to heat treatment. A centre for this trade is Bangkok, Thailand, where reddish-brown stones from the Indo-Chinese gemfields are heated to temperatures around 1000 degrees Centigrade and various techniques used to change the gems to golden-yellow, waterwhite and sparkling blues.

Old names used for the natural stones are hyacinth or jacinth for the orange-red to red-brown stones and jargoon for yellowish, grey or smoky stones. Heat-treated waterwhites are misleadingly called Matura diamonds.

Hardness is $6\frac{1}{2}$-$7\frac{1}{2}$ on Mohs' scale and indices of refraction are 1.92-1.99, all varieties being strongly doubly refractive. Main facet angles are 43 degrees for the crown and 40 degrees for the pavilion. A tin lap with Linde A is recommended for zircon, which is not an easy gem to polish. Most stones possess soft spots which can only be completed on a slower-running lap with powder that has been allowed to become almost dry.

Australia is one of the world sources of fine zircons. Waterwhites, yellow, red and brown stones of gem quality are abundant in the New England district of New South Wales and Victoria, where zircons are the commonest gemstones. Fine large stones are also found in Queensland, particularly on the Anakie gemfield and also in Tasmania. Ceylon produces fine zircons and other sources are India, Brazil and various places in the United States. S.G. varies from 4.0 to 4.82.

A notable absentee from the above list is the diamond. Because of their extreme hardness, diamonds are dealt with in different ways than other gemstones. First they are roughly shaped by cleaving or splitting and sawing and then preformed by bruting with another diamond. The stone is then faceted with diamond dust on an iron lap.

These are techniques which few hobby gemworkers are likely to attempt, owing to the value of the gem as well as its extreme hardness.

Expert knowledge is necessary to decide the best way to deal with a rough crystal. Sometimes as much as half the material may have to be cut away to get rid of flaws and produce the most profitable shapes or sizes.

Cleaving is carried out with a thin, blunt-edged tool known as a cleaving iron. This is applied parallel to one or other of the octahedral planes so that the crystal divides when the iron is struck a smart blow.

A diamond may be split in any one of four directions by this means or sawn from any one of nine other directions, all of which are laid down by the crystal structure of the gem.

These operations, together with bruting, are known as diamond cutting, while the process of faceting is described as diamond polishing. Polishing also may be carried out from only one direction and therefore the diamond polisher, like the cutter, must be a practical crystallographer.

In the trade, cleaving, sawing, cutting and polishing are all specialist occupations. Sometimes polishing is split up between two sets of workers, the most skilful of whom cut only the main crown and pavilion facets of the gem.

## COSTS

At the end of 1966, lapidary supply houses were offering faceting materials at the following prices: Amethyst, 44 cents to 6c. a carat; apatite, 25c; citrine, 12 to 15c; chrysoberyl, $1.50 a carat; emeralds, $20 to $5 an oz.; fire opal, $40 to $10 an oz.; hematite, 5c a carat; rock crystal, 50c an oz.; rutilated quartz, 13c a gram; sapphire, $90 to $10 an oz., $6-15c a carat; smoky quartz, 50c an oz.; spinel, $3.20 a carat; staurolite crystals, $2.50 to 30c each; synthetics (alexandrite, kunzite, ruby, sapphire, spinel) all 3c and 4c a carat; tektites, 10c to $1.25 each; topaz, 5c to 8c a carat; tourmalines, 50c. A carat weighs 3.086 troy grains, of which there are 480 to the ounce. There are 31 grams in an ounce.

These prices are, of course, subject to fluctuation and are not binding on any lapidary dealer.

# 6

## GLAMOUR AND GLITTER

WHENEVER MOST PEOPLE think of jewellery, they think of faceted stones. The glitter and sparkle of facets are the essence of the glamour that attaches to such words as jewels, gems or precious stones in the popular mind.

The art of faceting is the chrysalis between the grub and the butterfly. In this case the grub is the rough gemstone. This can take the form of either a jagged broken fragment or a dull waterworn pebble. Often little trace remains of the original crystal shape.

The greater part of faceting material is either clear or translucent. It is also likely to contain flaws of various kinds, some of which can only be seen with a magnifying glass. These flaws will consist of cracks, inclusions and sometimes bubbles of gas or water.

Quartz crystals sometimes contain bubbles of water. Other inclusions are usually mineral crystals of various kinds. Some gemstones, such as amethysts, frequently show patterns of tiny cracks. Other cracks, more difficult to detect, occur along the cleavage plane of the crystal and are only seen when the stone is turned in the light.

It is important that as many of these flaws as possible are discovered before work is commenced on the stone. Several devices are practised to assist the gem-cutter in spotting flaws, the most obvious of which is to grind and polish two or more opposite areas known as windows in the stone. The windows allow the interior of the stone to be examined with an eyeglass.

A more elaborate method which does not involve interference with the rough material is an immersion test. This consists of placing the piece of rough in a white bowl containing liquid with an index of refraction as near as possible to that of the gemstone.

The effect is similar to that of a piece of ice in water. The transparent

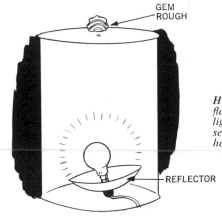

*How gem sculptor Ross Fraser spots flaws in his cutting material. A bright light inside a two-gallon drum is focussed into a strong ray through a nail hole in the top of the drum.*

solid almost vanishes while the ghostly traces of cracks and inclusions remain to be seen. By this means turpentine, with a refractive index of 1.47, allows us to look into fluorite (1.43) and oil of cloves (1.54) into iolite, which it exactly matches, and quartz (1.55).

Higher up the scale, however, immersion fluids are either expensive or poisonous or both. For this reason most gemcutters prefer to use a strong electric torch placed beneath the piece of rough. Although this does not show up flaws in structure and colour quite as clearly as the fluids, it is a lot more convenient.

A better method of examining rough used by Sydney gem-carver Ross Fraser is to place a strong light, such as a 120 watt bulb, mounted with a reflector inside a two-gallon drum. Mr. Fraser then inspects his material in the ray of light coming from a nail hole driven into the top of the drum. He says this method works with even the darkest of translucent stones.

It is only when flaws are seen that they can be assessed. Major flaws and weaknesses must be avoided. Minor imperfections such as small feathers can be hidden by cutting them into the girdle facets of the stone. Attractive inclusions can add to the beauty and interest of the stone if they are cut into the pavilion as we noted in the previous chapter. The best and deepest patches of colour should be similarly treated.

It is hard to give too much time to studying your gem in the rough. Remember that as soon as the first cut is made on the preform you are more or less committed to the final gem. This first cut is usually made on the trim saw and the object is to secure as large a stone as possible, consistent with the flaws you have seen.

Preforms for the two basic faceted styles—the step-cut and the brilliant—differ as soon as the flat area which is the future table of the stone has been cut. The step-cut preform is oblong while the brilliant, being round, is first shaped as a cylinder.

Shaping is carried out on similar principles to gem-carving, using the saw to get rid of as much waste material as possible. Final preforming is best done, not on the coarse grinder but on the 220 wheel. For a first gem, quartz is a good choice of material, either as smoky quartz or rock crystal. Work almost to the proportions of your finished stone.

This means that for a step-cut gem, you will aim at a rectangular preform of which the table is half the narrowest width of the girdle. This girdle measurement, in turn, is between twice and one and a half times the depth of the pavilion. If it exceeds these dimensions the stone will be either too wide or too deep.

The girdle is marked around the stone at one-third of the total depth from the table, leaving the remaining two-thirds as the pavilion. The sides of the pavilion are then bevelled towards a point and the edge of the table also bevelled towards the girdle. In each case be careful to leave a margin for final cutting.

Sometimes the step-cut is seen with facets at the corners which changes the shape of a cut-corner rectangle. Sometimes the corner facets are so wide that the stone becomes almost an elongated octagon. If it is intended to cut the corners, a start can be made on these facets on the preform but they should not be developed too greatly.

The main difficulty in the step-cut will be found in keeping the corners square and the sides precisely parallel. This problem is met by using templates and also by careful checking with a millimetre gauge which should be used on preforms of any shape.

Similar difficulties are met with the brilliant preform which should be as near to an exact circle as possible. When you have succeeded in forming a fairly well-shaped cylinder, dop that end of it which you have already cut as the table and put the finishing touches to the circular shape by turning the dopstick in your fingers as you continue grinding.

The proportions of a quartz brilliant are similar to those of the step-cut. The pavilion is twice as deep as the crown and the diameter of the table half that of the girdle. Mark the position of the girdle on the preform and continue grinding at an angle so that the pavilion is bevelled to a blunt point.

You can now fit the dopstick into your faceting head and cut the pavilion facets or alternatively transfer the dop and proceed to grind a bevel between the table and the crown. If you decide to transfer the dop, a transfer block or jig which holds both dopsticks rigid during the operation will aid in ensuring that the stone remains square on the dop.

Dopping cement used for faceting is harder and tougher than the wax used for cabochon cutting. Bear in mind that the harder and tougher the wax, the more difficult it is likely to be to remove the stone from the dop later.

Before starting faceting, let us examine some of the mechanical faceting equipment at present being used by amateur gem-cutters in Australia. Of these devices, the freehand head and the mechanical dop-stick are relatively simple and inexpensive compared to the fixed index heads.

All three types operate on similar basic principles to control faceting angles and the order in which facets are cut, although the cheaper implements offer greater scope for error as well as wider opportunities for craftsmanship. All three types of heads have so-called cheater devices that allow slight adjustments to be made when the stone is locked in place.

The popular type of Australian-made freehand head has an octagonal plate at the end of the dop-arm, which holds the stone mounted on a dopstick. This plate permits eight facets to be cut on a single index setting and three adjustments on the dop-arm provide for the cutting of a total of 32 facets.

One advantage of the freehand head is that it may be picked up at any time to allow examination of the gem because it only rests on the stand-rod and is not fastened to it in any way. Facet angles are set on this head by means of a protractor laid against the dop-arm while the stand-rod is raised or lowered.

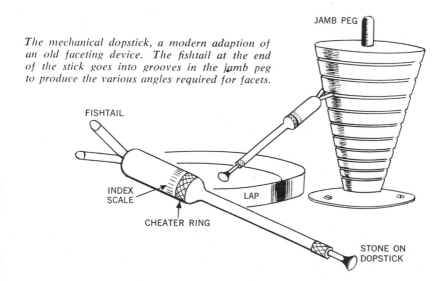

*The mechanical dopstick, a modern adaption of an old faceting device. The fishtail at the end of the stick goes into grooves in the jamb peg to produce the various angles required for facets.*

JAMB PEG

FISHTAIL

INDEX SCALE

LAP

CHEATER RING

STONE ON DOPSTICK

The mechanical dopstick is an ingenious adaption of the old jamb peg method by which professional lapidaries faceted gems for many years. The jamb peg is an inverted cone of hardwood with a series of holes in which the end of the dopstick is inserted in order to obtain the various facet angles.

A similar peg is used with the mechanical dopstick but instead of holes it has a series of grooves cut all round the peg, each a quarter of an inch apart. The dopstick consists of a device similar to the dop-arm of the freehand head. It is equipped with a fishtail, two metal blades in the form of a vee, which fit in the grooves of the peg.

The jamb peg then becomes a sort of stand-rod and by selecting different grooves the cutting angle of the dopstick is varied. Like the freehand head, these angles can be set up from a protractor. A scale of 32 index positions is provided around the shaft of the dopstick to any one of which the stone can be set and locked.

A cheating device is provided by means of a knurled ring beneath the scale which allows the crown and pavilion facets of a brilliant to be lined up precisely after re-dopping. Once set the correction is automatically applied to each facet as it is cut. The fishtail fitting locks the dopstick laterally in relation to the jamb peg, keeping each facet in line.

The dopstick is held to the lap in the fingers of one hand, usually the right hand, in the same way as the other faceting heads. Pressure against the lap controls the rate of cutting, but as with the freehand head, frequent examination of the stone is the only safeguard against over-cutting.

Dependent on the skill of the operator the mechanical dopstick allows more latitude in the number of facets cut around the gem compared to the freehand head, which is limited to squares and multiples of four.

Two of the most popular Australian fixed index heads are the Agate-master, made by J.F.W. Engineering of Brisbane, and the Gemmasta, manufactured at Richmond, South Australia. Both heads are basically similar in operation, but each has special features.

Fixed index heads have the dop-arm attached to the stand-rod by joints that permit up-and-down as well as to-and-fro motion. The former movement is controlled to some extent by the vernier or quadrant, the angle of which is varied by raising or lowering the junction of the dop-arm with the stand-rod. The vertical stand-rod or post may also be moved to-and-fro in relation to the lap, thus allowing slight variations of the cutting position.

The rotation of the dop-arm is controlled by the index wheel which

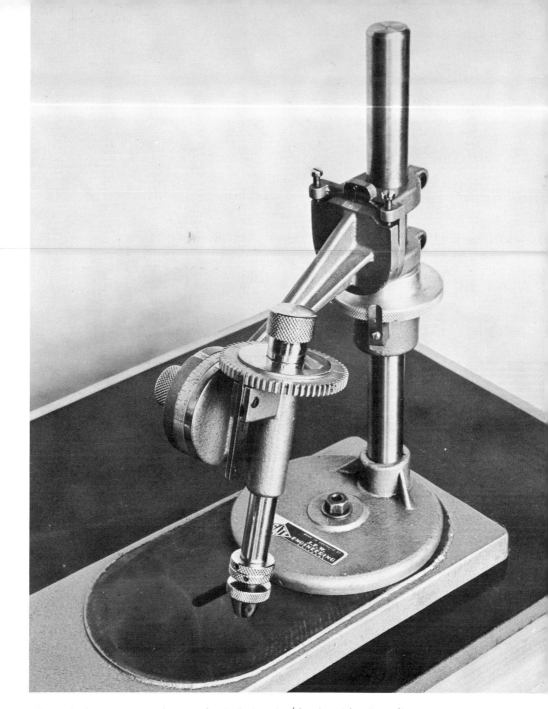

One of the most popular mechanical faceting heads with Australian hobby gemworkers is this 64-index Agatemaster made by J.F.W. Engineering, of Brisbane. Operation of this device, as well as four others, is explained and described in Chapter Six.

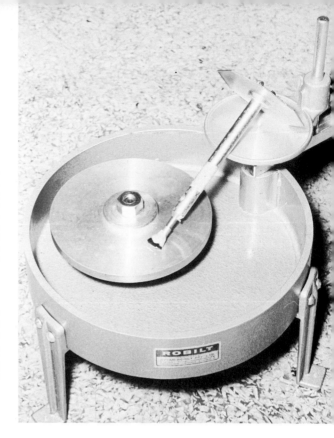

More Australian hobby gemworkers start faceting with the Robilt Gem Maker than with any other machine. This inexpensive Melbourne-made kit is equipped with the freehand type of mechanical faceting head.

Below: The popular Gemmasta 64-index faceting head set up in operating position. Dops, vee-dops and table-cutter are seen on the plywood base, with the transfer block on the right.

Above: A section of the Gemmasta machine's splashbowl removes so that the dop arm can be aligned horizontally with the lap surface and the girdle of the stone rounded by rotating the chuck by hand. Below: The method by which the table-cutter or 45-degree adaptor of the Gemmasta machine ensures the easy and precise cutting of the table of the gem.

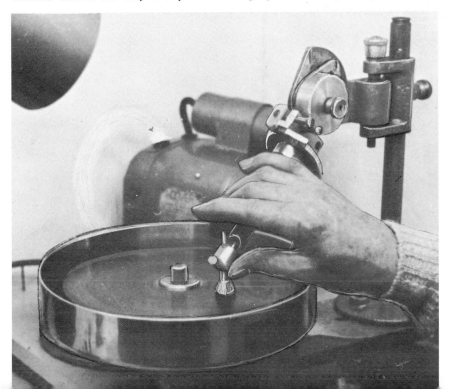

# HANDMADE JEWELLERY

*The excellent pieces of handmade jewellery on this and the following pages were entirely made by hobby artist-craftsmen of New South Wales, for the most part working in their homes.*

*The quality of this work illustrates more clearly than any words can describe the extraordinary degree of proficiency it is possible to achieve in these circumstances, given initial enthusiasm and the desire to create objects of lasting beauty.*

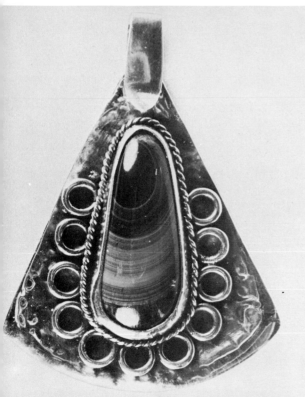

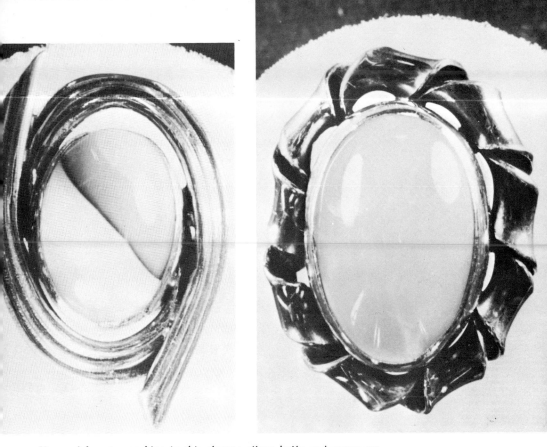

*Use and beauty combine in this elegant silver knife and spoon set.*

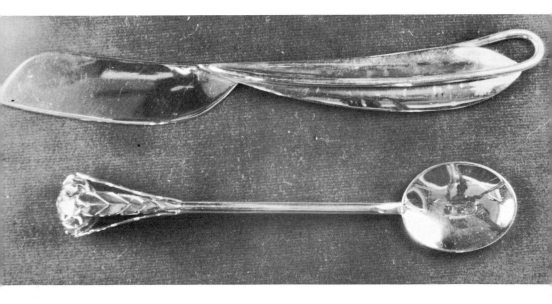

*The glamour of faceted stones. The size of these examples of various round and step-cut gems can be gauged from that of the hand holding them. This splendour is achieved using materials such as coloured and waterwhite quartz, aquamarines and topaz.*

in the case of both heads mentioned has 64 teeth or notches spaced evenly around the wheel. A trigger device engages and locks the notches as required, allowing any one of 64 facet positions to be selected on the stone. Variation of the quadrant angle controls the position of the facets vertically.

Both heads include several fine adjustments for cheating, both radially and heel-and-toe. The Agatemaster head has both rough and fine cheaters on the dop-arm. If a large nut at the top centre of the index wheel is slackened the spindle can be rotated with the trigger still in the gear. A screw and locking screw device at the chuck end of the arm allows fine adjustment or splitting of the indexing.

A similar device is sited behind the index trigger on the Gemmasta head. This consists of two thumb screws, the top one of which acts as a lock. A graduated scale above the zero line on the screws enables the cutter to split in either direction. The entire adjustment equals one tooth of the index gear.

Both heads have micrometer height adjustment which permits heel-and-toe cheating. This is incorporated in the vertical pivot of the Gemmasta machine and below the crosshead of the Agatemaster. The Agatemaster also has a little lateral adjustment on the crosshead that allows cheating on the diagonal facets of cross-cut or scissors-cut stones.

A popular feature of both fixed index heads are devices permitting the dopped stone to be removed from the head for examination and accurately replaced at any stage of cutting. On the Agatemaster head this is achieved simply and positively by providing the dopsticks with a chamfered end which slips under a lock pin in the chuck. On the Gemmasta the whole chuck complete with index gear is held on the dop-arm by a spring-loaded ball and can be slipped off for examination. The dopped stone need not be removed from the chuck, giving the Gemmasta a similar facility to that of a freehand head.

Angle stops are fitted to both heads. Two index marks on the Agate-master quadrant guide the gem-cutter on how far he has to go before the stop takes effect. The stop is set by locking the angle pointer at the required position on the Gemmasta quadrant. The dop-arm will not swing lower than this angle.

Both machines and also the freehand head described earlier are provided with a table-cutter or 45-degree adaptor. This adaptor facilitates cutting and polishing the table of the stone at exactly 90 degrees to the lap. It fits into the chuck on the dop-arm and itself has a vertical socket into which the dopped stone is inserted.

There is a slight variation in the methods of setting up this table-cutter. In all cases the dop-arm is set at a 45 degree angle. On the Gemmasta machine the head is then lowered until the table-cutter almost touches the lap. It is then further lowered by the micrometer height adjustment until the flat base of the cutter is seated squarely on the lap. The chuck is then tightened and only a slight height adjustment is necessary when the dopped stone is placed in the table-cutter.

The Agatemaster head has a face-plate dop which is inserted in the table-cutter. The face of this dop, which is mounted in the cutter in the same way as the dopped stone, is laid perfectly flat on the lap surface, thus ensuring that both dop-arm and cutter are set up correctly. The dopped stone is then substituted.

By using the table-cutter, suitably-shaped pieces of gem rough can be dopped and have the table cut and polished before preforming. The table then forms a useful window by which the stone may be examined for flaws before proceeding.

After cutting the table can be rounded or alternatively squared up on the Gemmasta machine. This is done after the dop has been aligned with index 64. The quadrant is then set to 90 degrees and the head lowered until the stone is just touching the lap. It can then be rounded by hand after the index trigger is disengaged or squared for a step-cut on index settings of 8-24-40-56.

So far we have outlined three different types of mechanical faceting devices and some of the special features of two makes of fixed index heads. Now let us see how these differences affect the cutting of the two basic types of faceted stones—the step-cut and the standard brilliant.

## CUTTING THE STEP-CUT

The step-cut was devised for coloured stones and indeed it improves their colour at the expense of brilliance. It is the easiest style to cut with either the mechanical dopstick or the freehand head, which requires no indexing, all the cutting being done on one setting of the eight-sided index plate.

The number of facets on a step-cut depend upon the proportions and size of the stone, but in general two rows on the crown and three on the pavilion are enough for all except large. stones, which might have three rows on the crown and four or five on the pavilion. The angles of these facets increase in steps to the girdle. Steps of large stones might rise by five degrees but 10 degree steps are more practical for smaller stones.

As the recommended main angles for quartz are 45 degrees on the crown and 43 on the pavilion, you begin by cutting the girdle facets either on the pavilion at 65 degrees or on the crown at 40 degrees according to which way the stone is dopped.

Dopping is carried out on a vee-dop if you have one. This is a dopstick with a vee-shaped notch in the end. Dops for brilliants have a cone-shaped hollow end. The wax and spirit-lamp are manipulated in a similar way to dopping cabochons and the wax should not reach quite to the girdle.

Indexing on the fixed head will depend on whether you are cutting a rectangular stone or a cut-corner rectangle. For the former it is simply 8-24-40-56 repeated, but for the cut-corner stone 8-16-24-32-40-48-56-64 for four rows and 8-24-40-56 for the final row on the pavilion.

Similar settings on the 32-point scale of the mechanical dopstick would be either 4-12-20-28 for the five rows or four rows of 4-8-12-16-20-24-28-32 and then 4-12-20-28 on the pavilion.

The point about first cutting the girdle facets is that you can make sure the girdle edge is true all round. The second cut on the pavilion is made at 55 degrees and the third at 45 degrees. The second row of crown facets is cut at 30 degrees.

When all the pavilion facets are cut and polished, you have to re-dop the stone before you can go on to the crown. For this you must have a transfer block in order to set the stone squarely on the new dop. Special transfer blocks are supplied with both the fixed index heads described, together with dopsticks of various sizes.

The transfer block has screws to clamp the dopsticks on either side. The old dop is inserted on one side and secured while a blob of hot wax is heated on the new dop. Often several attempts are necessary before the new dop is secure. The two sticks are left in the transfer block to cool. The old dop is then removed by careful heating.

The method of cutting steps sounds easy written down but in practice your first step-cut gem may give some trouble, most of which will be due to the preform not having been prepared carefully enough. The secret is the girdle. Providing that is level and true, you cannot go far wrong.

Polishing begins on the row farthest from the girdle and is continued working towards it. Cheating devices on the fixed index heads are useful in putting right those facets on the long sides of the stone that polish unevenly.

## CUTTING THE STANDARD BRILLIANT

Of all faceting styles, the brilliant is the one which most amateur gem-cutters want to attempt. Cut with the correct angles of inclination for the gemstone in question, it will give almost total reflection of light and really lives up to its name.

The main facets of a quartz brilliant are cut at 45 degrees. The best method of cutting these facets with either the mechanical dopstick or the freehand head is to start by cutting the first, fifth, third and seventh facets in that order. This produces a square around the table and if this square is imperfect, the cutter will be able to see any inaccuracy clearly. Once this has been put right, the four remaining main facets can be added.

Indexing for this procedure on the 32-point scale is 4-20-12-28 followed by 8-16-24-32. On the freehand head you merely have to switch from side to side of the eight-sided plate. All main facets must be of equal width. Cutting to a square on the fixed index heads is achieved using index 64-32-16-48 in that order, followed by 8-40-24-56.

The crown should now be a symmetrical octagon with the girdle line clearly defined. To cut the star facets, the mechanical dopstick is raised a couple of grooves on the peg and the facets cut on an index of 2-6-10-14-18-22-26 and 30.

The freehand head is put on the 16 index and the dop-arm set to 30 degrees. The fixed index heads are also set to this angle and indexed 4-12-20-28-36-44-52 and 60. Star facets are very small and hardly require more than a touch on the lap.

For the 16 break or girdle facets, the mechanical dopstick is dropped three or four notches and indexed 1-3-5-7-9-11-13-15-17-19-21-23-25-27-29-31. The freehand head is set on the 32 index and adjusted to an angle of 47 degrees. The fixed index head, at the same angle, is indexed at 2-6-10-14-18-22-26-30-34-38-42-46-50-54-58 and 62.

The stone is then polished, stars first, then mains and finally the girdle facets. After transfer dopping, the pavilion is cut, first eight mains at 43 degrees and then 16 girdle facets at 45-47 degrees, the indexing for these being the same as the crown mains and girdle facets. Pavilion girdle facets sometimes cause a little trouble through over-cutting. They must all be exactly the same depth. Polishing is carried out on the same index and angle settings, mains first.

## DIAMOND-CHARGED AND OTHER LAPS

Modern facet cutting is mainly carried out on diamond-charged copper laps. These laps may be mechanically charged, in which case the lap is expensive because about 2 carats of diamond dust will be embedded in it. If you prefer you can buy a copper lap and charge it with diamond dust yourself.

Special packs of 20-40 micron dust are prepared by Diamond & Boart Products (Aust.) Pty. Ltd. for gem-cutters. This dust is mixed with a grease applicator so that it can be rolled into the surface of the lap with a hard steel tool. A coating of oil on the lap helps to spread the diamond dust.

The other side of the lap is usually charged with an extremely fine polishing grade of diamond dust. This 0-2 micron compound is dyed a distinctive colour and is rolled into the lap surface in a similar way. The lap should first be scored with the point of a knife. Hand-rolling will get about half-a-carat of dust into the surface.

A good deal of time and grief will be saved for learners if they invest in a small set square and use it to ensure that their stones are always dopped square to the dopstick. A tilted stone cannot be cut true and its girdle facets will not meet correctly.

Girdles should never be cut and polished to a knife-edge because this edge is certain to chip when set in a claw setting. If the dop-arm can be lowered to a horizontal position, the girdle should always be rounded before polishing. Failing this, the dopstick can be removed and held in the fingers to round the girdle.

Get into the habit of keeping the stone moving from side to side as you cut or polish to avoid wearing a groove in the lap.

Cleanliness is most important when faceting to prevent contamination of laps. You should wash your hands, your stone and the chuck of the faceting head whenever you change laps. Clean paper should be placed between the working lap and the master lap, especially if the working lap is double-sided. Clean out the splash pan each time the lap is used.

The lap surface must be kept moist during cutting. This is usually done with a wet sponge in the left hand or a wet sponge placed on a length of wick fastened to the edge of the splash pan and laid across the lap. The lap must never be allowed to run dry. The heat from a dry lap would probably ruin your gem.

Never point the dop-arm into the spin of the lap. There is every chance that a corner of the stone might gouge the lap surface and the stone itself could be ripped off the dop. Always place the stone on the lap so that it trails.

Of the many different types of recommended polishing laps you will do well to possess a lucite lap (with tin or cerium oxide) for quartz; a tin lap (with tin oxide) or a boxwood lap for many gems and a spare copper lap (with tripoli) for sapphires.

The metal laps must all be scored to hold the polish which is applied to the lap as a weak solution by means of either a sponge or a cotton cloth.

Many variations of the brilliant cut are seen, some with horizontal split main facets and others with vertical split mains. The three-quarter brilliant possesses only eight girdle facets on both crown and pavilion. Both the step-cut and the brilliant are modified into many shapes and also combined as mixed cuts.

As you grow more experienced, two cuts worth attention are the cross-cut or scissors-cut, which resembles a step-cut with long triangular facets, and the lens cut, a modern shape, which has a series of long narrow facets on a cylindrical stone, bevelled at each end and step-cut on the back.

(The information on which this chapter is based was provided by Mr. Jack S. Taylor of St. Leonards, N.S.W., Mr. A. F. Schluter of J.F.W. Engineering, Newmarket, Brisbane, and Mr. R. A. Gaerth of Gemmasta Lapidary Equipment Company, Richmond, S.A.)

## COSTS:

Taylors Little Gem freehand faceting head and support, $17; mechanical dopstick, $17, jamb pegs, $2. Robilt freehand faceting head, $11.50. Gemmasta faceting unit (laps extra), $170. Agatemaster faceting machine with motor, mounted on wooden table (no diamond dust), $270; without motor and table, $198; faceting head only, $120.

Laps, copper, 6 in. $1.75; 8 in. $5 to $18; 10 in. $8; 8 in. diamond-charged both sides, coarse and fine, $22; 8 in. tin, $15-$18; lucite, 6 in. $1.05; 8 in. $6; Perspex, $6. Diamond dust, $4.50 to $6 a carat; syringe pack, 2 grams compound with grease base, $6.50.

These prices were quoted at the end of 1966, and are subject to fluctuation. They are not binding on any manufacturer or lapidary dealer.

# HOW TO CUT A CHINESE TEMPLE

While Major George Owens was running a lapidary business in Seoul after the Korean War he had an opportunity to examine Chinese temples at first-hand and at the same time to discover the methods by which Chinese temple gems are carved.

Major Owens, a former U.S. air force officer, passed on this information to me not long ago. He came to Australia in 1959 and now has a gem business in West Ryde.

Chinese temples are best cut from the finest quality rock crystal. Size is entirely up to the cutter and depends on what you can obtain. The stone should be transparent and flawless.

The piece of rock crystal is first cut on a diamond saw to a tapered prism shape. This is an equilateral triangle, 20 to 30 degrees larger at the base than the top. Height depends on the thickness of the crystal, but if the prism is too long and thin it is likely to be broken.

A vertical flat about half the width of one side of the prism and nearly two-thirds the total height is now ground across one of the angles on a silicon carbide wheel. This now becomes the back of the stone. A

*The behaviour of light within a faceted crystal is used by Oriental gem carvers to produce these Chinese temples. A series of cuts on the back facet appears as a pagoda in perspective when seen through the front of the stone.*

BACK

SIDE

FRONT

facet of 30 to 40 degrees is cut across the top of the prism pointing to the back flat and tiny relieving facets run up the entire edges of both remaining prism angles. This safeguards against chipping.

The whole is now sanded and polished according to normal quartz techniques before a start is made on carving the temple. This enables the carver to watch his progress and make any necessary minor improvements as he goes along.

Carving is done on the trim saw and consists of a series of graduated notches cut into the triangular flat at the back of the stone. The width, depth, thickness and number of these notches will depend on the dimensions of the stone and the carver's wishes.

The first three notches are cut deepest and close together at the base of the prism like three steps. This forms the base or foundation of the temple. The next five or six notches are progressively finer and smaller and gradually spaced closer together. Each notch represents a tier or storey in the building, with the widest space and the broadest and deepest cut following the deep cuts at the base.

This should bring you almost to the apex of the flat. Another six or eight tiny notches are now cut along the back angle of the prism towards the apex of the facet cut across the top of the stone. These notches form the spire at the top of the pagoda.

Sanding and polishing these notches is the most difficult part of the task, says Major Owens. He uses a skewer sharpened to a pencil point and dipped first in olive oil and then in 600 grit as his sander. He slits the pointed end of another skewer, inserts a few strands of cotton wool and uses that as a polisher wet and dipped in cerium oxide.

Larger notches can be sanded and polished on knife-blade rock hard felts of the type used by jewellers. Be careful, however, because these felts generate a good deal of heat and may damage your stone.

Finally take a diamond point and make markings between the notches to represent walls and doorways. Add touches at the ends of each notch to represent the typical carvings at the ends of pagoda roofs. Then give the whole piece a final sparkling polish.

This basic carving method dependent as it is on the reflections of light within the prism, can be adapted to various shapes. The illustration shows a peardrop prism cut by an Oriental carver. The dimensions are $1\frac{1}{4}$ in. by $\frac{7}{8}$ in. The face has been cut slightly convex to increase the optical effect and the pear shape cleverly superimposed on the prism.

If you want to do something special in the Chinese temple line, perhaps as a gift, get the largest size boule (about 240 carats) of synthetic ruby, sapphire or spinel, advises Major Owens. This will not shine as well as rock crystal but the colour looks very good.

A boule this size will cost about $9.60 to $7.20 at present prices but you will have sufficient left over for several faceted stones if you saw carefully.

# 7

# QUEEN OF CRAFTS

### by Laurel Gorn

OF ALL CRAFTS, jewellery-making is the most absorbing and exacting. It can also be the most rewarding. Almost everyone at some time or other feels the urge to creative craftsmanship. Our primitive ancestors have left plenty of evidence of this same urge, which too often is stifled in modern life; but which, if it can only be encouraged and fulfilled, gives feelings of happiness and satisfaction that nothing else can.

It is because of the richness of these rewards that jewellery-making has been called the queen of crafts. It is not a cheap hobby; yet, on the other hand, it need not be too expensive for a person of average means who restricts the buying of tools and equipment to keep pace with the increase of proficiency and experience.

Initial tools are neither numerous nor costly. The item that requires most thought is the blowtorch for this is one thing on which it pays in the long run to spend a little more. A mouth blowpipe which is used in conjunction with a spirit lamp or Bunsen burner is the least costly. This device takes some practice to fully control and still leave both hands free although many professional jewellers still prefer it. Another inexpensive little torch is the Davi-Jet, which can be attached to ordinary domestic gas fittings with a length of rubber hose and is successful with small pieces. However, the flame of this jet cannot be regulated.

Several kinds of gas blowtorches are available and are generally used by professionals but the type most widely used by hobby workers at present are propane gas torches. The cheaper of these are powered by replaceable gas cans, while the type that is more expensive to buy, but more economical to use, is lit by refillable gas cylinders. This torch costs almost three times as much as the other initially, but the first-named is at least seven times more expensive on gas. From the figures given at the conclusion of this chapter you may work out for yourself which is the best for your own needs.

Next on the list is a non-inflammable mat, such as a half-inch or quarter-inch thick asbestos sheet. If you have to work on a household table, use a twelve-inch square over a piece of board or a number of thicknesses of newspaper. The board does a better job in preserving the table from damage. Supposing you are fortunate enough to be working on a bench, a smaller asbestos mat is sufficient or the traditional charcoal block is excellent although its working life is shorter than that of asbestos.

JEWELLER'S SNIPS            ROUND-NOSED PLIERS            CHAIN-NOSED PLIERS

You will require few tools at first but make sure they are the best available. You will need two pairs of pliers, one flat-nosed and the other round-nosed, and they should be bought from a jewellers' suppliers. The usual hardware store pliers are not meant for use with precious metals.

Other essentials include: One pair of six or seven-inch steel tweezers;
One seven-inch flat file of medium cut;
Two needle files, one knife-edged and the other half-round;
One pair of six or seven-inch tinsnips with fine blades;
One jeweller's saw frame and one dozen size 3/0 blades—the range of blade sizes extends from No. 2 coarse to 8/0 extremely fine, but these are enough for the present;
One small ball peen hammer;
One very small cold chisel, slightly blunted;
One pair of steel dividers, about four-inch are large enough;
One wooden bench pin, this is a piece of plank 3-4 in. wide by 6-7 in. long, with a vee cut, used in conjunction with a suitable metal or "C" clamp;
Old knitting needles, both steel and plastic in various sizes;
A steel block such as the bottom section of a disused electric iron;
Emery paper, both fine and medium grit;
A brass brush, of the kind sold by bootmakers, for brushing up the work after soldering is completed.

More tools will be needed as progress is made, but providing you have the items listed above, a start can be made.

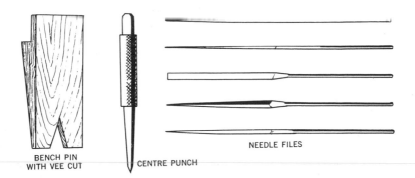

BENCH PIN
WITH VEE CUT      CENTRE PUNCH                      NEEDLE FILES

Working facilities are simple—as much light and ventilation as possible and a good working surface. A garage which boasts a workbench in a good light is ideal, of course, but some hobby workers, particularly housewives, have to make the best of the kitchen table.

Lay down plenty of newspaper to protect the table. It is as well to cover the whole surface so that you can spread out your tools. Another advantage is that when you have finished all the mess is in the newspaper, so you can just roll it up and throw it in the garbage can.

Working in the kitchen, or for that matter, wherever you are working, care must be taken to keep chemicals out of reach of the children. It is necessary to use a diluted solution of sulphuric acid, known to jewellers as "pickle", and this must be clearly labelled and marked "POISON".

Any diluted sulphuric acid should be kept under lock and key in a glass bottle with a glass stopper, clearly marked. It should never, never be left lying about.

The pickle itself is less dangerous, being a solution of one part acid to nine parts water, although this is enough to rot your clothes or take off paint and varnish if you should happen to be careless and spill it.

If you mix your own pickle, bear in mind one important fact—always add the acid to the water and never on any account water to acid. Keep some washing soda ready to apply at once if acid splashes on your clothes or furniture. Use baking soda if any gets on your hands or face. However, it is safer to get your chemist to make up the solution for you.

Pickle is essential to clean the work after heating. Sterling silver goes black when heated and this black oxide or fire scale has to be removed by placing the work in the pickle once the red glow has faded and then rinsing it in clean water. So the jewellery worker must have a bowl of pickle and a bowl of water ready whenever the blowtorch is in use. You also require a pair of copper tongs, which can be made from strip copper, because your good tweezers will soon be ruined if you use them to put your work in and out of the pickle.

Another essential chemical is the flux. Flux prevents the surface of the metal oxidizing during soldering.

The cheapest flux is borax—the common borax you buy at the hardware store is better for soldering than the pure quality sold by chemists. The borax is mixed with a little water and painted on the work with one of those small watercolour paint brushes you can buy for a couple of cents. There arc also rcady prepared fluxes for silver soldering on the market.

Of all the metals used for jewellery-making, silver and gold are the most rewarding with which to work. Both metals are generally used as alloys for jewellery purposes, silver usually being alloyed with copper and gold with silver and copper. Gold coloured white, green, blue, red and other colours is obtained by alloys with various metals. Gold alloys are expressed in terms of carats, a carat being the unit of purity, and pure or fine gold is 24 carat. Standards for gold alloys available in Australia are 22, 18, 14 and 9 carat, although the composition of the alloying metals may be varied.

Sterling silver, which is an alloy of 925 parts of fine silver to 75 parts of copper, is the metal mostly used. Gold should not be attempted until the worker has learned to solder well and has a thorough understanding of metals and control of tools. I do not advocate first working in copper because this metal has a much higher melting point than silver—1083 deg. Centigrade as against 961 deg.

The learner who becomes accustomed to working in copper has to make a considerable adjustment in soldering techniques before tackling silver, whereas if you can work in silver successfully, you will have little difficulty with copper and gold. Gold, owing to its cost, is not widely used by amateurs. In buying gold, gold solder of the same carat must be purchased with it, but silver solder can be used for copper.

Silver is bought from a metallurgist or jewellery supply house at a price of so much a Troy ounce, either in the form of wire or plate. There have been so many requests by hobby jewellery-makers in recent months that at many places now silver is sold by the square inch in plate or by the foot in wire. This is a great convenience as most beginners don't know how much silver there might be in an ounce.

Wire may be bought either round, square or half-round. Both wire and plate is sold according to standard gauges. As there are several of these gauges and the result is apt to become confusing, thicknesses are sometimes expressed in decimal points of an inch, which is perhaps the better method. Tables of the Standard Wire Gauge, used for both wire and sheet silver, are published as an appendix to this book.

You will find that the suppliers stock the popular gauges of both wire and plate and that anything out of the ordinary will have to be ordered specially. Knitting needles are a great help to women in estimating what the thickness of a certain gauge of wire would be. Knitting needles and wire gauges are very similar although, of course, the wire gauge decreases to much smaller diameters than those of knitting needles. Generally, however, the beginner will not want anything thicker than an 18 and 20 gauge wire, both available round and square.

Manipulating wire is one of the basic skills to be learned in jewellery making although it is not the first. Before wire can be worked, it must be annealed. Before annealing, it is necessary to know how to handle the blowpipe or blowtorch.

The mouth blowpipe takes a little practice to use properly. Air must be inhaled through the nose, stored in the cheeks and then slowly expelled through the blowpipe. Once this knack is learned, it is possible to obtain a very delicate control over the flame. The harder you blow the stronger and hotter the flame will be.

Before any metal either wire or plate can be shaped to a desired form it must be annealed to take the spring out of it. Annealing is a process of heating the metal until its internal structure is changed and stresses are removed. The requisite piece of plate or coil of wire is laid on the asbestos block and a gentle heat played on it with the blowtorch. Silver should be treated cautiously especially in fine gauges and not heated beyond cherry-red which appears as a soft pink glow in daylight. Sterling silver melts at 893 deg. Centigrade, which is 68 degrees below the melting point of pure silver.

Fine wires can be annealed in a tobacco tin over a hot plate or gas jet. Wire is coiled for annealing in order to avoid the risk of melting. When annealing wire, it is most important that the torch flame should be kept moving all the time. The flame must be played around the coil smoothly and evenly and the finer the wire, the gentler the flame. If the heat is concentrated on any particular spot there is a danger of burning or melting the metal.

A burn mark on silver is a black blemish that will seem to disappear in the process of pickling. But as soon as you start polishing, the blemish returns as a dark cloud. This is not noticeable on a small textured piece or on wire, but anything larger, such as a spoon bowl, for instance, can be badly marked.

One way of preventing a burn mark is by constant dipping in a solution of hot and strong boracic (boric) acid. Boracic acid can be bought from any chemist. Burn marks can also be eradicated by dipping the piece in a strong solution of nitric acid and then scouring it with emery paper. This treatment may have to be repeated several times before the mark disappears. Nitric, of course, is another dangerous acid that should be handled carefully.

Annealing should be carried out whenever it is necessary to change the shape of a piece of metal. Remember that red-hot metal is weakened—gold, for example, is likely to break if it is moved while red hot. As soon as the colour fades, the article can be popped into the pickle solution with the copper tongs to be cooled or quenched and cleaned at the same time. (Gold under 14 carat must not be dipped into cold liquid when hot but allowed to cool in its own time. If you are working against time, it can be cooled in methylated spirit.)

Having a modest tool kit and a knowledge of basic processes, a start can be made on your first piece of jewellery. If working in silver, the result can be something of value.

*To make a simple pendant, inner and outer bezels of fine silver are shaped and fitted together. Then a filigree of silver wire is soldered in place and finally the top rim of the bezel is turned over the edge of the cabochon stone.*

A good first piece might be a pendant of a simple enough design to be finished in one lesson and pretty enough, providing the work has been done carefully, to be worn afterwards with pride.

If you are cutting your own stones, you will want to set one in this pendant. Choose a cabochon not larger than one inch but not smaller than half an inch in diameter.

You will need a strip of fine silver plate in 28 gauge for a very small stone or 26 gauge for a larger one. First measure the stone to determine the length of silver required for the bezel, which is the metal setting that will grip the edge of the stone when it is set. Cut a piece of paper about ¼ inch wide and measure the exact circumference of the stone by winding the paper around it and marking the join in pencil. Then take your dividers and, holding the stone in front of your eyes, find the height required for the bezel.

Naturally a high cabochon will need a wider strip than a low one. The ideal stone has sides that slope well from the base. A stone with too steep sides is difficult to set.

For the type of setting you are making, an inner bezel will be needed and so this must be allowed for in the width of the outer strip. This must be the width of the inner strip, plus just enough to bend over the stone to hold it securely. If the design you plan calls for a high set stone, the inner bezel is cut high, for this is the piece on which the stone rests. If the stone is to be set low, a very thin inner bezel is needed; a length of thin wire will do.

Having determined the length and width of your outer bezel, measure off your paper strip on the piece of fine silver plate. Then take the width from your dividers, scribing a line on the silver with one of the two points while the other is kept against the edge of the metal. You can now cut off this strip.

Your strip now could be correctly described as a collet. Collet is the name given to the ring of metal which encircles the stone in a setting and the bezel is that part of the collet which secures the stone in position, although in general use the two terms have become synonymous to some extent.

The strip is now laid on the asbestos pad and annealed by heating until the metal glows pink. Fine silver does not discolour like sterling silver under heat and so your strip only needs to be cooled in the water.

The annealed metal can now be wrapped around the stone as easily as a piece of paper. The two ends of the strip must neither leave a gap nor overlap, but meet precisely. Any overlap is easily adjusted but if the strip is too short, the only thing to do is to lay it aside and cut another.

As soon as the collet is snugly fitted to the shape of the stone, the ends, which must meet exactly, are carefully filed to make a good join before being soldered. All jewellery soldering in precious metals is what is described as hard soldering. This is a different process than the use of tin and lead alloy soft solders. Hard soldering is carried out at red heat and the metal being soldered is almost at melting point when the solder melts. Consequently fusion takes place and the join becomes part of the whole.

The strip, now shaped into a circlet, is placed join downwards on the asbestos pad and heat first applied on the opposite side to the join. If this is not done the two edges of the join will spring apart and a good join will be impossible. This technique of heating on the opposite side of the join applies when any circle is being joined. The heat softens the metal so that there is no stress remaining to draw the ends apart.

In silver soldering the heat is never applied directly to the part to be soldered. When soldering a large piece of metal to a small one, the heat must be played mainly on the larger piece. Once the large piece is hot enough, the small piece will heat with it and the solder will make a good join. But if the small piece of silver is allowed to get too hot, all the solder will run to it and will not make a strong join.

Silver solder is made of alloys of fine silver and brass in several grades which melt at temperatures between 800 and 725 degrees Centigrade. The lowest temperature solder is the easiest for the beginner to handle. Solder can be bought in both wire and sheet form in various gauges. It is prepared for use in the sheet form by snipping the solder into squares of about one-sixteenth of an inch known as paillons. These paillons are mixed with the borax flux solution before use.

Parts to be joined must be thoroughly cleaned before being painted with flux, using the water colour brush. One or more paillons of solder— the number naturally varies according to the size of the piece—are placed along the join with the brush. The work is then heated in the manner previously described until the solder flows into the join and fuses on both ends of the strip.

When the solder melts the flame is removed for a second and then quickly returned until the solder is seen to run into the join. A soft flame rather than a fierce one is needed for successful soldering. The hottest part of the flame is just off the blue tongue. The flame should not be applied suddenly, but held well above the work and slowly lowered as the flux dries until the tip of the flame barely touches the piece.

As soon as the work loses its red heat, it is dipped in the pickle, rinsed with water and any excess solder removed with a file. Never flatten excess solder by hammering. This results in unsightly marks if the piece has to be heated again, causing the solder to run where it is not wanted or eat into the silver.

When the outer bezel or collet is completed, the inner bezel on which the stone will sit is measured and cut from fine silver plate. This inner bezel is joined in the same way as the outer one and then soldered into place. It should be a tight fit. Then file the underside of the circlet smooth, rub down on emery paper and clean up around the bezel, especially over the join. If this has been soldered well, it can be made invisible.

As soon as they are soldered into circlets, both outer and inner bezels should be tested to see they are the correct size. If either proves to be too large, it will have to be cut and joined again. If either is too small, it can be stretched a little by placing it over a ring mandrel or a piece of suitably-sized dowel. The bezel is then struck and tapped all round with a wooden or rawhide mallet. Very little tapping is needed to stretch it. Before both bezels are finally joined together another test is made to see if the stone sits too high. If so, the inner bezel must be filed down a little.

A simple and attractive form of decoration around the bezel is a filigree of, say, 20 gauge silver wire. Wind an annealed length of wire round a knitting needle, coiling it closely like a spring. The coil of wire should be long enough to reach about two-thirds of the way round the bezel. After removing the coil from the knitting needle, take hold of each end and stretch it so that there is equal space between each turn of the coil.

Now lay the coil down on the table and flatten it with the fingers. When partly flattened, it can be rolled with a piece of wooden dowel or even a rolling pin. Anneal the coil, then form it into a circle and solder the join. This can now be stretched over the bezel like elastic. Press it well down and solder in place.

This particular filigree is one of the best for a first attempt, being neither too difficult nor too easy. Soldering will present the greatest problems and it will probably be necessary to repeat the process, adding more solder.

If the coiled wire leaves room for it, a fine twisted wire also can be soldered around the bezel where the flattened coil meets it. To make the twist, double a piece of annealed 24 gauge round wire, clip the two free ends in the jaws of a vice and slip a knitting needle into the bend of the loop thus formed. Then, holding the wire taut, turn the knitting needle hand over hand until the wire is tightly twisted.

Anneal again and measure off enough to fit around the bezel. This should fit snugly. Join it and fit it well down on the coiled wire. Place very thin pieces of solder round it—not too much—and heat it until the solder melts and runs.

Finally, make a small ring by turning a piece of 20 gauge wire around the round-nosed pliers. Thread one end of this ring through a loop of the coil and solder the join of the ring with a tiny snip of solder and a very low flame. In this case it is not necessary to play the heat over the rest of the piece but try to keep the flame on the opposite side of the little ring to the join at first.

It is sometimes helpful when soldering wire to use a solder paste. This is made by mixing solder filings with the borax flux and applying the mixture to both surfaces to be soldered with the brush.

When soldering is completed, the work is brushed up under a running tap with the brass brush. This restores the shine to the silver. The piece must be filed free of any tool marks. Then the file marks are removed with emery paper.

Lapidary hobbyists who are fortunate enough to possess power tools can fit jewellery polishing buffs to their machines for the finishing processes. These are buffs made from discs of soft cotton stitched together which can be bought at any jewellery suppliers. Although it is likely to be unpopular advice, I suggest that every learner should polish his first pieces of jewellery by hand. Polishing by machine demands practice because the work may be very easily whipped out of the hand and damaged.

If the pendant is to be finished by hand, powered tripoli and rouge are required. Tripoli is a finely pulverised silica rock while rouge is fine iron oxide. Both are used mixed with grease in cake form for machine polishing. For hand use the powder is mixed to a paste with a little water in a saucer.

This paste is then rubbed on the work with a soft felt brush or small strips of felt or lambswool and hard rubbing is needed to produce a smooth polish. When all the fine scratches of the emery have been removed by the tripoli, the pendant is washed in hot soapy water with an old toothbrush and then rinsed clean.

At this stage the work can be given what is known as the antique finish. This gives the piece an attractive bluish-black tone which is the accepted finish for an article of handmade silver jewellery. This is done by dipping the pendant into a hot solution of potassium sulphide or liver of sulphur. It can be bought from most chemists in lump form by the ounce. A piece of this chemical about the size of a pea in a pint of hot water makes a strong enough solution. The pendant is left in this solution until it turns bluish-black.

It is then rinsed under the tap and polished with a paste of powdered rouge and water. This paste is applied in the same manner as the tripoli but, of course, using fresh strips of felt or lambswool. The work has to be rubbed up hard so that all the highlights are really bright and well-polished while the sunken parts remain dark.

If necessary, the more intricate parts of the filigree can be polished with strands of wool or cotton treated with the appropriate polishing mixture which are threaded through the aperture to be polished and then vigorously rubbed to and fro. This procedure is called trumming.

When polishing is completed, the work is washed again in hot soapy water and scrubbed with the toothbrush, rinsed in very hot water and dried while still hot. It must be dried at once because if it is left to get cold, the polish is likely to become smeary. It is at this stage, when everything else is completed, that the stone is set in the bezel, although hard gems such as agate can be set before polishing if preferred.

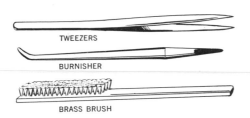

TWEEZERS

BURNISHER

BRASS BRUSH

To set the stone, seat it on the inner bezel and press down the upper edge of the outer bezel with a burnisher or the back of the pliers or any tool with a smooth rounded surface.

If the cabochon is oval start at the ends, first one and then the other, then the sides and stroke the metal from the ends to the sides. The polished surface of your tool will burnish the bezel as you stroke it round and over the stone. Put a fair pressure on it and the stone will be secure. The pendant can now be hung from a chain by means of the small ring.

The flattened coil filigree is just one pleasing and easily-made example of the multitude of jewellery designs which can be formed from wire. Work in wire is perhaps the first thing that the handcraft jeweller should attempt. It is both inexpensive, interesting and instructive. No more tools are needed than the jewellery pliers and the fingers, once the wire has been annealed.

Properly annealed wire should bend and twist like string and it can be knotted like string as well. So-called lover's knots in thicker—say, 12 gauge—wire can be the basis of simple and effective rings, brooches or pins. These designs and a wide variety of scroll, spiral and twisted units can be produced without soldering, but once the latter technique has been mastered, the possibilities with wire become infinite.

However, wire requires a lot of practice before the learner achieves a really smooth finish. Every time the pliers are pressed on a piece of silver wire they leave an unsightly mark. Therefore the right way to handle wire is to hold one end in the pliers and do most of the twisting and shaping with the fingers.

At first the majority of learners cannot resist an urge to reverse the process. They take hold of the wire in one hand and start shaping it with the pliers. It is, of course, essential that the wire should have been well annealed beforehand. Unless this is done properly the wire will be too springy to bend smoothly and difficult to control.

Good wire work requires practice and the learner is advised to purchase a coil each of 18 and 20 gauge copper wire and use his or her ingenuity in making as many different units as possible. Scrolls and figure-S shapes are difficult at first but perfect forms can be made with practice. Copper is much more pliable—and very much cheaper—than silver.

Copper wire is also useful to find the length of wire required for a design. After forming the design to your satisfaction in copper, the wire can be straightened out and a piece of silver wire cut to the same length. It is often easier to work out a design in copper wire than to make a sketch of it on paper.

Twisting different shapes and gauges of wire together opens up another series of possibilities. As well as its more obvious uses for drilling holes, the hand drill offers a means of twisting wire neatly and evenly. To do this a small cup hook is secured in the chuck of the drill and the wire to be twisted is doubled over the hook with the loose ends secured in the vice. A perfect twist of wire is then obtained by turning the handle of the drill.

When twisting heavy wires, the cup hook may not hold so it is better to slip a steel mandrel or a strong steel knitting needle into the bend of the wire and twist by turning the mandrel hand over hand. The wires will require annealing two or three times before a tight twist is achieved.

Many variations of twists can be made and can be used for bangles or to make decorative units for other jewellery items. For instance, 12 gauge square wire, well annealed, can be twisted with a fine round wire, previously twisted itself, to produce an attractive bangle. Before an even twist is achieved these wires may have to be removed from the vice several times and again annealed at sections which have not twisted evenly.

A strip of plate can be twisted alone or with a round wire. Square wire can be twisted alone. When twisting separate wires a pair of strong pliers will have to be used as there is no loop which can be twisted.

Complicated designs in wire can be formed on a jig. A jig is made from a flat piece of soft wood and some panel pins. The design is first drawn on the wood and the pins tapped into it with a hammer so that the ends protrude. The wire is then twisted around the pins and slipped off when the design is completed. Any heads on the pins should be removed before the wire is shaped around them. The completed design may need soldering at certain points if it is to decorate a bezel or form a piece on its own.

Finally these wire patterns can be soldered on plate and combined in the most delightful way as flowers and leaves, stalks and vines with other patterns punched, stamped or forged in the metal. But that is another chapter.

## COSTS:

A mouth blowpipe can be bought for about 25 cents, a Davi-Jet complete with rubber hose for 73 cents, a gas can blowtorch for $5.50 complete and one of the gas cylinder type for $15.28 complete. Extra cans of gas cost 65 cents each and refilled cylinders around 30 cents.

An 8 in. by 8 in. asbestos mat costs 40 cents, a charcoal block 50 cents, flat-nosed and round-nosed pliers each $1.69. The total cost of the essential tools listed is a little over eight dollars, a brass brush costs 29 cents and the metal for copper tongs 12 cents.

The price of sterling silver wire varies from $1.30 a foot for S.W.G. No. 12 to 5 cents a foot for No. 26. Square wire varies from $1.80 a foot for No. 12 gauge to 22 cents a foot for No. 20. Pure silver wire of No. 18 gauge costs 30 cents a foot and No. 19, 22 cents. Sterling silver sheet varies from 91 cents a square inch for No. 14 gauge to 15 cents for No. 32 gauge. Pure silver sheet costs 20 cents a square inch for No. 28 gauge to 15 cents for No. 32.

A three by one inch sheet of easy silver solder costs 30 cents and a similar amount of hard solder 33 cents. Tripoli costs 69 cents a bar and rouge $1.25 a bar. Polishing buffs cost 95 cents for rouge and $1.15 for tripoli. Annealed copper wire costs 18 cents a coil.

The prices quoted were current at the end of 1966 and are subject to fluctuation. They are published as a guide and, of course, cannot be regarded as binding on any jeweller's supply house.

# 8

# SETTINGS AND SHAPES

## by LAUREL GORN

IF YOU ARE A LAPIDARY, you are likely to have some stones you want to set. Start off with cabochons, not with baroque or tumbled stones. In the last chapter, I described how to make a simple pendant setting for a cabochon. Now a ring can be made by similar methods.

Select a cabochon, not larger than half an inch. Make your bezel as you did before, only a little higher than for the pendant.

Having measured the stone and determined the height of the outer bezel, cut a strip of 26 gauge fine silver sheet in these dimensions. Then cut the inner bezel, also higher than you did for the pendant. It could be at least half the width of the outer bezel, perhaps even higher.

Join the two bezels separately, test with the stone and make certain the inner bezel fits very tightly. If the inner bezel is too high to allow the top edge of the outer bezel being turned over the stone to secure it, either file it or reduce it by rubbing on a sheet of emery paper. Do not solder the bezels together until you are satisfied that the fitting is correct.

Take two lengths of 20 gauge square wire which will form the shank of your ring. These wires must fit around the finger and also be carried round the bezel, each wire forming half the enclosure for the bezel. The wires must be soldered together while they are still in the flat and for this you will find iron binding wire most useful.

Binding wire can be bought in reels at jewellers' suppliers and is used for binding parts together for soldering when no other method will hold them close enough. It should always be removed before dropping the piece into the pickle or it will discolour the silver.

Tie the two wires together in the centre and then put a tie on each side of that, but leave the ends open for about half an inch, pulling them apart slightly to prevent the solder running right to the ends which will later be fitted around the bezel.

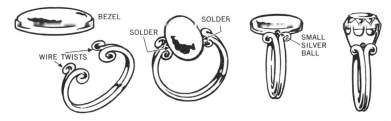

*Shoulders for a ring setting are made by twisting the ends of two strands of 20 gauge square wire forming the shank. The result is effective with either cabochon or faceted stones.*

Your ring size now has to be marked in pencil on a ring mandrel. This size is obtained by wrapping a strip of paper around the finger on which the ring will be worn and transferring this size to the mandrel by fitting the paper around the tapered shaft at the point where the ends of the strip meet.

Now bend your soldered ring shank around the mandrel above the pencil mark and slide it down to the mark. The bezel must now be fitted exactly between the square wire ends so as to keep the size of the ring.

To do this, the four ends are spread out, while the ring is still on the mandrel. The ends must lie at right angles to the ring shank and flattened along the mandrel. Now fit the bezel between the four ends spreading them further or closing them as necessary until they fit close to the bezel. All this is done at the marked size on the mandrel.

The two sides of the square wire will touch the bezel only in one spot and this must fit very closely. Remove ring and bezel from the mandrel and now that you know the size is correct, you can squeeze the sides of the shank a little closer together so that when it is placed over the bezel again it holds tightly like a spring.

The shank ends should be kept as close to the bottom of the bezel as possible and if they fit tightly, the ring can then be stood upside down on the bezel. A touch of solder is placed at each join where the square wire meets the sides of the bezel and the flame played gently over the whole piece. The bezel should now be secure on the shank.

You are left with four free ends of square wire and these can be either snipped off where they are soldered to the bezel or they can be carried round the sides of the bezel until they meet (while doing this, keep the stone in the bezel or it will go out of shape). The ends then can be mitred to fit and—after taking out the stone—soldered in place together with the wire around the bezel.

On looking at the underside of the bezel you may find that its edge is a little lower than the square wire holding it in place. So take a half-round file (larger than a needle file if you have one) and file the underside of the bezel so that it forms a curve conforming to the shape of the shank and makes a complete circlet.

Having made the underside smooth, you can consider a surround for your stone. Often a circle of fine twist wire is all that is needed, but you may prefer a little more decoration—say, small leaves soldered on either side of the shank. Four leaves will be enough, two for each side with a little ball at the centre of each. Where the square wire meets the ends of your bezel, you could perhaps solder a very tiny ball.

Small balls or shot are best soldered to a piece by filing the solder and mixing it with a little flux to a paste. Dip the balls into this and place them where required on the fluxed piece. Several balls can be soldered together in the same way as, say, a bunch of grapes. This method of soldering can also be used for fine filigree work.

You may have to put your ring back on the mandrel and tap it with a wooden mallet to restore it to perfect shape. Brush up, emery and polish the piece and set the stone as I described in the previous chapter.

When setting an oval stone, always turn the ends of the bezel over first. The reason for this is that if the sides are turned over first or you start at one side and go all round, you end up with a bubble or pleat in the metal. Stroke round the bezel very carefully so that your burnisher does not slip over on to the stone.

Finally, you may have to take a needle file and slightly file off the top of the bezel as this can become a little uneven in the course of setting the stone. Careful filing with your finest file will put this right.

A clear faceted stone will need a claw setting and the simplest of these is made by similar methods to the closed setting you have just completed. Make your shank in the same way as you did for the cabochon and also make your bezel in the same way only very much higher.

You have to allow for the claws and also for the height of the faceted

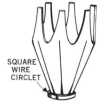

SQUARE
WIRE
CIRCLET

*A simple form of coronet is made by snipping out points in a tubular bezel, bending these points inward and soldering them in a circlet of silver wire.*

stone, which tapers to a point underneath. This point must not reach below the bezel. Therefore you must measure this carefully and allow plenty of metal for the height of the stone. Measure the stone from the table to the point or culet because you must allow that much extra for the claws.

Then an inner bezel must be cut. The inner bezel should measure in width from the girdle of the stone to the culet which will leave just enough of the outer bezel to form the claws. Having fitted and soldered the two sections of the bezel securely together, seat your stone in it to see that you have enough height. If the outer bezel happens to be too high, don't worry about it at this stage because you will be cutting away most of the outer bezel to leave claws.

Most round faceted stones have six claws. Take a pencil and mark the outside of your outer bezel into six equal spaces. Leave plenty of room. Make the claws much wider than their finished shape.

Now snip down the sections between the claws as far down as the top of the inner bezel. Draw the cut sections out a little so that they can be cut off and filed smooth. This should leave six little sections upstanding which you will later file down to claws.

Now you cut away the lower part of the bezel. Using your piercing saw, take vee-shaped pieces from the bottom of the bezel reaching almost to the top of the inner bezel. This leaves six little pointed legs. Smooth and even these up with a file and emery paper. Place the stone in the bezel and draw these legs slightly under to conform more or less with the tapered shape of the stone.

See that the legs are very evenly spaced and when you are satisfied you have them all correct, remove the stone and rub the legs down with emery paper so that they all stand level.

Make a tiny circlet of square wire just large enough to solder on to the six little legs. Rub this down with emery, then sweat solder the circlet to the bottom of the legs.

Sweat soldering is the safest method of attaching all small pieces to your work without the solder appearing where it is not wanted. The small piece, in this case the circlet, is placed on the asbestos mat and tiny fragments of solder laid on with flux. Play the heat on the circlet until the solder melts.

Flux the ends of the little legs, reflux the circlet and place it in position. Lower the torch flame carefully so that the circlet is not displaced by flux bubbling up. Play the flame evenly round the bezel until the circlet settles into place. Watch carefully for this as you will not see the solder run.

In sweat soldering it is very important to ensure that the little pieces do not heat before the larger piece to which they are being soldered.

Sweat soldering is also used to applique one piece of plate over another or a textured piece to a plain piece or plate over wire. Plate solder is best for most sweat soldered pieces but, if you have none, flatten small wire solder pieces with the hammer on a steel block.

Sweat soldering the circlet completes your bezel which is now a simple version of a coronet setting. When it is attached to the shank, the four free ends of square wire can be curled back individually to form shoulders with perhaps a small ball or a pair of tiny leaves soldered in the angle. Alternatively the ends can be cut off and the shank soldered directly to the square wire circlet at the bottom of the bezel. You can then add shoulders in the form of leaves or a wire pattern if you wish.

A great variety of gemstone settings can be handmade but they require much experience. The smaller they are, the more difficult they can be, as even the slightest imperfection is noticeable. It is therefore necessary to practice bezel and collet working as much as possible. Both must fit the stone perfectly.

*A coronet setting is made from two pieces of fine silver cut as parts of a circle and folded into a bucket shape. Six prongs or claws are cut from this bucket to hold a faceted gemstone.*

CORONET SETTING: The crown or coronet settings require great care and time. It is best not to make one at all rather than do it badly.

Most coronet settings are started as a bucket-shape and to form this shape the bezel must be cut in a curve. The best way to do this is to describe a circle on a piece of paper and take one section which, if cut out, will fit exactly around your stone.

The easiest way is to measure round your stone with a strip of paper and curve this around the circle you have drawn, marking the measurement of your strip of paper on the circle.

Scribe a line from each side of this section down to the central point of your circle. This will give the angle at which to cut this piece. It forms a triangular segment with one curved side. This curve should fit exactly round the girdle of your stone.

Measure the depth of collet you require from the top of this curve. Cut this off following the line of the curve and you should have a curved strip the length and height of your collet with the correct angles for the join.

This paper pattern is cut out in 20 or 22 gauge fine silver sheet and the ends brought together and soldered. You will now have a perfect bucket shape to fit your stone. Cut out claws as you did for the previous setting and file away an equal section on the inside of each claw to form steps on which your stone will rest.

This collet can also be made with an inner bezel. This bezel must then be cut at the same time as the outer bezel, forming exactly the same curve. This is soldered down to the outer bezel in the flat and formed to the bucket shape. In either case the collet must be pierced to allow light to reach the stone.

TIFFANY SETTING: The Tiffany is a modern and popular setting, well within the scope of the amateur. You will find it easier to cut an enlarged pattern from cardboard before attempting it in silver.

For the pattern use a halfpenny or a 10 cent piece in place of the faceted stone. Lay the coin on the cardboard and mark on each side of it with the scriber. From these two dots rule two lines to form a vee-shape. On either side of the lines draw two more lines so that your vee becomes a quarter of an inch thick.

Cut out the vee and use it as a pattern to make another one exactly like it. Cut halfway down the apex of one vee and halfway up the apex of the other. Insert the second vee inside the first and push the cuts into each other until the points of the vees are level.

Now cut little nicks about one-sixteenth of an inch down on both sides of the inside of each vee and level with each other. Fit the coin into the four slots. If it does not fit enlarge the slots carefully until the coin slips into position. It is far easier to fit the coin into the cardboard pattern than the stone into metal.

For your first setting choose a fairly large faceted stone and cut another cardboard pattern, this time actual size. Be careful not to make the nicks too wide. They must slope slightly up and down to follow the slopes of the stone so that the nicks grip the edge of the girdle. If the upper line of the slots is too high, they will stand away from the stone and there is nothing you can do about it, so take great care to get them exact.

When you are satisfied with your cardboard pattern, cut the two vee

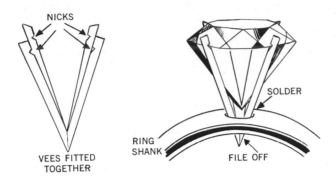

In the Tiffany set-
ting, two vee-shapes
cut in sheet silver
grip the girdle of
the faceted stone.
The tip of the vee is
soldered into a hole
in the shank of the
ring and filed level.

shapes in 20 or 22 gauge sterling silver sheet. Allow for any irregularities in cutting by making the inner side of the vee slightly smaller than the pattern and do not make the vees too long.

Make the cuts at the apex of the two vees very carefully with the piercing saw. After the saw cuts have been fitted together, stand the piece upside down on the table and tap with the hammer until the points are level. Solder the join.

A strong way to attach this setting to the ring shank is to drill a hole at the join and push the point through solder and file away the protruding point. Alternatively you can file down the point to get a good flat which you can then solder to the shank.

Often nothing more is needed although shoulders can be added as long as they do not reach more than halfway up the sides. Before setting the stone, file the tops of the claws down if necessary, keeping them level with the table of the stone and just below it. If the claws are too wide, file them down from the outside. Clean up well and polish.

To set the stone, carefully turn the top of one claw sideways with the flat nosed pliers. Slip the stone into place and turn the claw back again over the stone to correspond with the other three.

For polishing the inside of rings, hard felt finger-buffs can be obtained to fit machine shafts. Use one for tripoli and another for rouge.

GIPSY SETTING: This traditional setting is often used with men's rings. The ring is usually cast and then scorped or bored to fit the stone to be set. For this special tools are necessary, chief of which is a scorper. Considerable practice is needed to manipulate the scorper. Metal is worked over the stone to secure it by a setting tool that has to be tapped with a hammer.

A setting like the gipsy can be made by casting the hollow for the stone a little larger and inserting a bezel, which can be worked over the stone with the burnisher, like an ordinary closed bezel setting.

Mock gipsy settings can be made by fitting a domed piece over a ring form sloped to take it and cutting a hole in the top of the dome in which a bezel can be soldered.

Bought cast settings can be incorporated in handmade pieces but most amateur jewellers prefer to make their own and leave the more elaborate cast settings to the professional. Gallery wire can be bought by the foot from metallurgists and made into bezels. This is already perforated and cut into tiny claws, but it has a decidedly mechanical look which goes badly with a handmade piece.

ADJUSTABLE RING: Often one is asked to make a ring and the size is not given. In this case the shank can be made adjustable. A very simple one is formed from a seven-inch length of 16 gauge round wire. Anneal the wire and flatten one end to form the free end of the shank. This can be pulled out or pushed in to fit any finger.

Holding this flat end down on the mandrel, twist the wire around the mandrel. Carry the end past the flattened wire and across itself at right angles to the shank. Then pull the wire round to form a seat on which to solder a bezel or perhaps a claw setting for a clear stone. If necessary cut a section off, but it depends on the size of your bezel how much wire you will need. You may have to use all of it, but finish it off by flattening the free end and this should tuck away underneath the spiral.

You can make the bezel in the normal way or if you want to make claws, cut three or four short pieces of 20 gauge wire, flatten each one slightly in the centre, then lay them across one another so the ends splay out like a star. These are your claws.

Flux and solder where the wires cross. This will leave a rather lumpy section in the middle but if you take the ball end of your hammer and hammer this down well it will flatten so that the join is almost indiscernible.

This can be soldered down on the slightly flattened section of the spiral of the adjustable shank. File the ends of the claws to a blunt point. They are turned up over a baroque or clear stone and will hold it quite strongly.

This ring can be made in a very short time and is useful at Christmas when gifts are needed for friends.

By this time you have added at least a ring mandrel, a wooden or rawhide mallet and a hand drill to your original tool kit. Other useful items you may consider buying are extra files, doming punches and a doming block, a centre punch and a set of ring sizes.

But there is no need to buy everything. Tools for texturing can be made from assorted sizes of nails, small cold chisels and screwdrivers. My first doming punches were made from old motor-car valves. Doming punches can also be made from short lengths of steel rod, the ends of which can be shaped on an old silicon carbide wheel. The sharp edges of cold chisels should be blunted slightly with a file and the sharp points rounded.

CHASING: Chasing and texturing of the metal can do much to lift a piece of jewellery out of the ordinary rut and give it life and interest, but the elaborate chasing and engraving of the 18th century is not popular today. What few chasing tools are necessary can be easily and cheaply made as I have already explained.

Sets of chasing tools can be obtained at a jewellers' suppliers and experiments with these can be of absorbing interest. For deep chasing and repousse work, jewellers' pitch in a bowl is used, but for most modern requirements the lead block is quite good, while for beating and lining only a thick piece of linoleum over the steel block is necessary, especially for small pieces like flowerettes and leaves.

Interesting patterns can be formed with the chisel punch. In the case of a flower or leaf, lines can be sunk into the metal which is then turned over and punched up to form petals and so on. Tiny leaves are formed by cutting a sheet silver strip into diamond shapes, veining them with the chisel punch, then turning over and ball punching them.

Effective designs are achieved by simply beating an annealed shape with the ball end of the hammer over the lino or lead block. This beating tends to concave the metal and sometimes this is desirable but if not, the piece can be turned over and flattened with the hammer face.

DOMING: The doming block has a number of round hollows of different

*This cute little fish cut from a silver plate provides a fine exercise in the use of doming block and punches. It makes an attractive brooch, too.*

sizes to be used in conjunction with the ball punches. To shape an annealed disc into a dome, place it in a hollow slightly wider than the disc's circumference, choose a punch which fits the hole easily and hammer on it until the disc is pressed well into the base of the hollow.

If the dome thus formed is too shallow or too wide, place it over the next smaller-sized hollow and select the punch next in size. Reduce the size of the dome in this way until the right size is reached.

If, in the first place, the disc is placed over a smaller hollow than its own circumference, the sharp edge of the hollow will cut an unsightly ridge around the plate. Small domes are used for setting pearls or can be used for decorative purposes.

Before beating metal it must be well annealed after sawing out the shape. Flowers, leaves, animal and fish shapes or free-form designs can be given a three-dimensional appearance by chisel or dome punching. First one side and then the other is beaten until the desired depth is reached. As beating progresses, the metal hardens and must be annealed again. Otherwise it will not shape up or it can crack or break.

USE OF THE PIERCING SAW: Sawing requires a little practice. A small piece of copper sheet might be tried before you first tackle silver. A bench pin, which is your piece of wood with a vee cut, is clamped to the table edge and the plate laid over the vee.

To fit a blade into the saw frame place the end of the frame against the edge of the table and press the handle against your body. Hold the blade at right angles to your body and run your thumb up it. If the teeth can be felt against your thumb, the blade is the cirrect way up. Place one end in the frame and screw it in tightly. With your body pressed hard against the saw handle, screw the other end of the blade tightly in place.

The blade should be as taut as a violin string. Grease it with beeswax.

While sawing, the blade should be kept perpendicular and the weight placed on the downward stroke. In shaping, the metal itself is turned rather than the saw.

When turning or cutting into corners, the saw must be kept moving, but pulled slightly back as the metal is turned; otherwise the blade will break. The saw should not be pushed but allowed to eat its own way through the metal.

SOLDERING HINTS: Apart from the use of binding wire, previously mentioned, the need to clamp sections together for soldering often arises and call for ingenuity.

Soldering tweezers can be bought and, although these are good, they often add difficulty to the task as the tweezers themselves must be hot before the silver will reach the required heat to melt the solder. Too long a delay in melting will cause the silver to oxidise instead.

I have found the humble bobby-pin the most successful clamp. It can be bent into any shape and will heat quickly. Split pins are also good but do not keep their spring as well as bobby-pins. Bobby-pins are also useful as props and supports and so are broken pieces of asbestos.

When you feel you have your soldering well under control, try a quicker method. Take a length of wire solder about 9 in. long. Heat the piece to be soldered to red heat, then touch the fluxed end of the solder wire to the join. Do not hold it there or it will form an unsightly blob. Then play the heat over the join again until the solder runs.

FUSING: When you are thoroughly conversant with the usual methods of jewellery making and have a full understanding of the reactions of metal under heat, fusing can produce fascinating results.

Interesting textures can be made by overheating the silver. Fluxed pieces of scrap metal can be laid over each other and fused together. The metal becomes molten and the heat is removed when the desired pattern is achieved. No soldering is needed.

Fine, heavy or twisted wires can be fused to plate and strips of sheet silver twisted, bent or folded and heat played on it until a sculptured effect is produced. Patterns can be grooved into a charcoal block or piece of asbestos, bits of silver laid in the grooves and fused.

Gemstones or pearls can be set in fused pieces with striking effect.

FORMING SILVER BALLS: Forming silver balls is one of the simplest tasks in jewellery making. Just put the tiny scraps of metal down on your asbestos pad and keep the flame of your torch on them. There is no need to move the flame at all, keep it steady over the scraps with just the tip of the blue flame touching, and the metal, whatever shape it might be, will run into a ball.

Don't try to make the balls any larger than say, a quarter of an inch, because even at that size they will show pits and marks. If you are making a larger-sized ball, dip the piece in flux first; this eliminates the pits to some extent.

If you want a number of balls exactly the same size, coil a piece of wire around a knitting needle and cut the coils with your saw. The circlets produced, being the same size, will run up into equal-sized balls.

Making balls is a good way to use up the scraps which by this time you will have collected and is more economical than cutting into a good piece of wire. Keep a small screw-top jar handy in which to drop every snipping as you work.

Silver, being a fairly expensive metal, should never be wasted, even

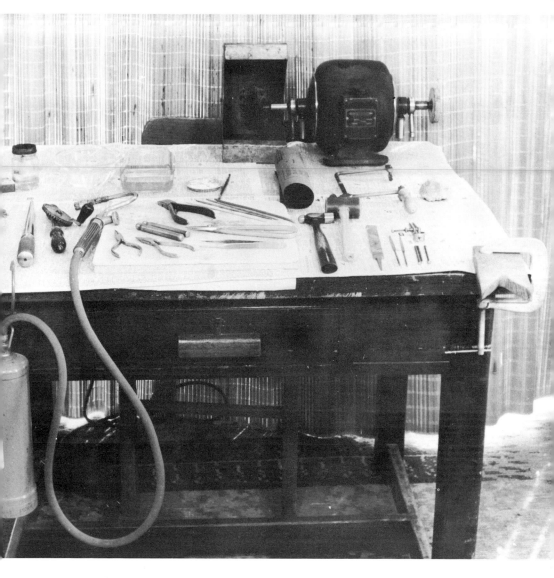

# JEWELLERY-MAKING

*Picture lessons in jewellery-making. First of all, the tools must be
laid out ready to hand before you settle down to work. Clearly seen
above are the blowtorch, bench pin secured by means of a clamp
and the buffing machine in the background. Mandrel, drill, saw,
files, hammer and mallet are among the other hand tools on view.*

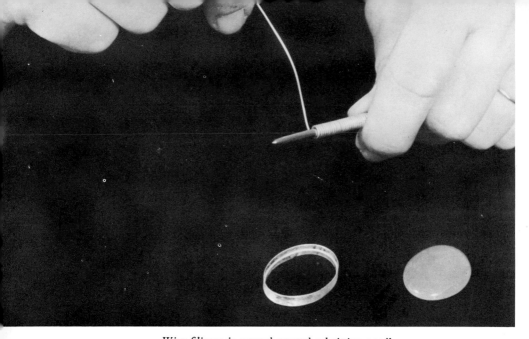

*Wire filigree is wound around a knitting needle.*

*When sawing, remember to turn the metal and not the saw.*

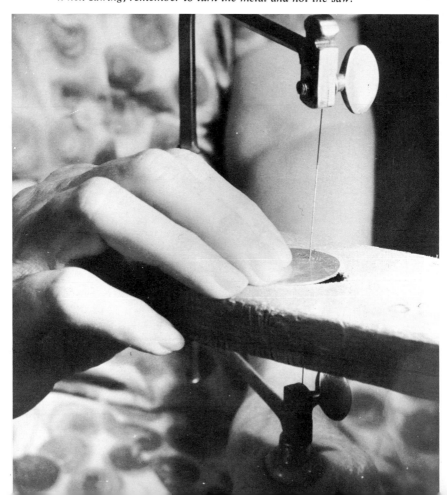

*Annealing . . . keep the torch flame moving over the wire.*

*The pendant described in Chapter Seven.*

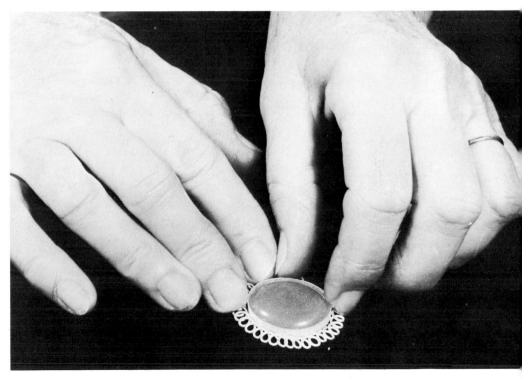

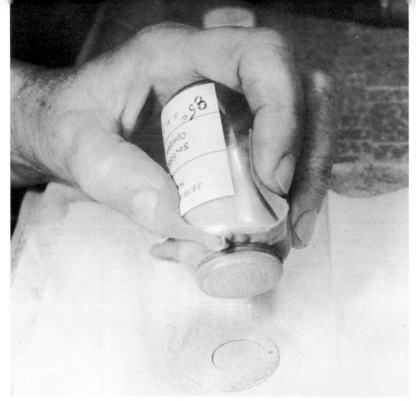

*Dusting powdered enamel over a piece.*

*Heating enamel with the blowtorch.*

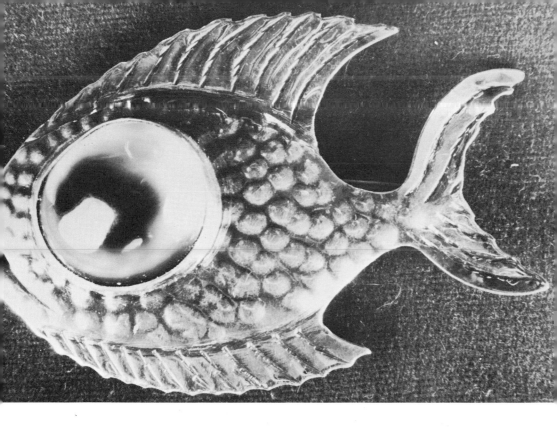

# DESIGNING
# IN SILVER

*All the examples of design shown here are the work of amateur silversmiths. Symmetry, balance and proportion are allied with much painstaking practice in the basic skills and in the use of tools. Hard work and enthusiasm are the secrets of success.*

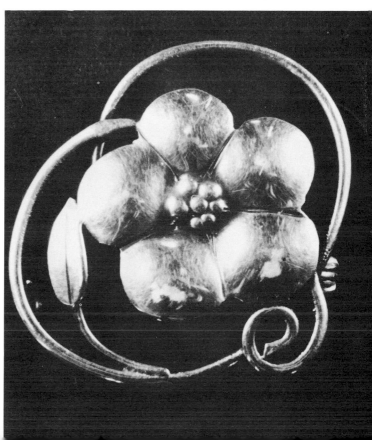

*Beauty in simplicity . . . and enlargement only
discloses the flawlessness of the craftsmanship.*

*Design from nature contrasts with (below) design from abstract shapes and textures.*

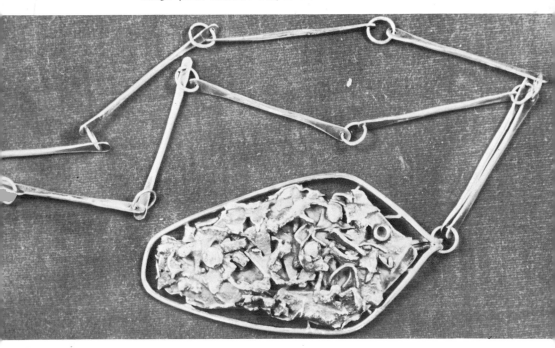

the tiniest pieces being collected and stored away. When your jar becomes full, you can take it to the metallurgist, who will buy back this scrap.

DRILLING ROUND OBJECTS: Sometimes it is necessary to drill a hole in a pearl or silver ball. This can be done in a jig. Take a strip of 16 gauge copper or aluminium plate and bend it in half lengthwise.

At the open ends of the jig, drill a hole or series of holes to fit the spheres you wish to drill. These holes should be too small to go right over the sphere. Drill the holes right through both thicknesses of metal.

Now open up the jig and, using a ball punch, punch into each hole causing the sharp sides of the holes to taper over the punch. Clean up and smooth these tapered sides well. Bend the metal and bring the two sets of holes closer together again.

Make a sliding sleeve of metal to fit over the double strip. When the sphere to be drilled is placed between two of the matching holes, slide this sleeve up to act as a clamp holding the sphere firmly in the tapered holes and between the sides of the metal strip.

CHAIN-MAKING: Links of exactly the same size to be used in chain-making are made by winding annealed wire closely and evenly around a steel or plastic knitting needle.

Take as many turns as you require links. Remove the coil from the knitting needle and then disconnect one end of a medium fine blade in your piercing saw and thread it through the coil of wire. Grease the blade well with beeswax.

Holding the work over a cloth or tissues spread over the table to prevent the links rolling off, saw carefully through the coil and the links will drop off the blade. If the wire is heavier than 20 gauge, the coil can be held in a ring clamp or in the jaws of a vice protected with a piece of leather or felt.

To open the links do not pull outwards as this will spoil the shape, but draw the ends apart sideways. Half the number of links can be soldered singly and then slipped on the remaining links to be soldered into chain.

Use the tiniest pieces of fine gauge wire solder that you can snip for the joins or the links may seize together. Do not forget the rule about when joining a circlet to play the heat on the side opposite the join.

Oblong links are made by coiling the wire around narrow strips of steel, but as this coil is difficult to slip off the flat steel, wind a strip of paper around it first. When the wire is coiled anneal it all, steel and all, and the paper will burn away. The coil is then easily removed.

Many types of fancy links can be made, such as figures Ss linked together with round links or round and oval links made of twisted wire.

Short pieces of square or twisted wire can be cut and round links soldered at either end. Short strips of plate or heavy round wire flattened at each end can be pierced and joined with links.

USE OF THE DRAW PLATE: As you progress, you may feel the need for a draw plate. A small vice is also needed to hold the plate and a strong pair of pliers or draw tongs to pull the wire through it.

Although wires can be bought in any gauge, a draw plate is useful to draw down short lengths of heavy gauge wire which might be too short to serve any useful purpose. Their length can be stretched up to ten times and their gauge reduced to 24 or 26.

Sometimes you may be out of a gauge of wire you need in a hurry and a draw plate will enable you to extrude a heavier gauge down to the size you want.

The end of the wire to be extruded must be sharpened to a long, tapering blunt point, as the draw plate holes are tapered. Of course, the

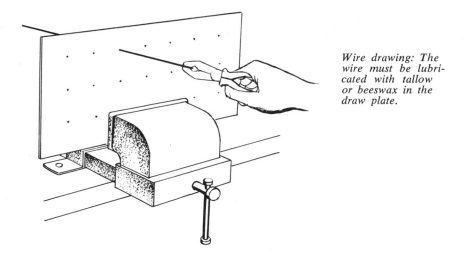

*Wire drawing: The wire must be lubricated with tallow or beeswax in the draw plate.*

wire must be well annealed and greased before drawing and repeatedly sharpened, annealed and greased throughout the process.

Tubing also can be made by drawing a strip of thin sheet metal through the holes of the draw plate; the finer the tubing, the narrower the strip. The end of the strip must be cut as a long blunt point to allow it to be inserted in the holes of the plate, with enough of the end protruding on which to get a grip.

The strip must be bent U-shaped along its length before inserting in the draw plate and this is done by laying the strip over a grooved steel plate and tapping it along its length with a rivetting hammer.

I find a good method is to place the strip over the slightly opened jaws of the vice with a steel knitting needle along it and tap the needle with a flat hammer until the required U-bend is made. You have to move the strip along as you tap.

Anneal the metal well, grease it and starting in the largest hole of the plate gradually reduce the size until the two sides of the strip meet. Should the tubing still be of a larger gauge than you require keep drawing it through the holes until it is reduced to the gauge you need. After the sides of the strip meet, continued drawing down will lengthen the tubing.

Tubing can be used to link bracelet sections or to make brooch catches or box snaps. It can also be cut up and soldered to sheet metal to give a coarse, rough look.

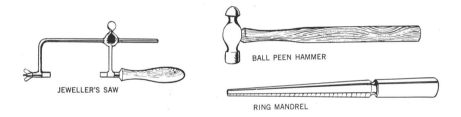

JEWELLER'S SAW

BALL PEEN HAMMER

RING MANDREL

CARE OF TOOLS: Care of your tools should be a very important consideration. Files, in particular, want special care and should be used correctly. They should never be put in with the other tools but stored separately, if possible in a grooved box—each file lying in its special groove—or in a block of wood with holes in it so that the files can be stood on end.

When using the file, always put the force on to the forward stroke. If you scrub away at a piece of metal as you would with a scrubbing brush, you will soon blunt the file. If you always put the force on to the forward stroke, which is the cutting edge, your file will simply sharpen as you go, but if you put the force on the backward stroke, you will only blunt and wear down the little teeth.

The hammer, too, is very important. As time goes on, you will find that this will pit slightly and if you rub it down on a piece of fine emery paper, you will eliminate these pits. But if it becomes badly pitted, you will find that each time you beat a piece of metal it will be badly marked.

All your tools should be kept bright. Pliers get very stained and if not cleaned up occasionally will soon rust. Damage to the jaws of your pliers is almost certain to affect your work and emery paper should be used to keep them smooth and shiny. A piece of worn emery paper, not a new piece, should be used to clean up tools and all stains and marks rubbed off with this.

The ring mandrel is very important. It should never be allowed to rust or become marked. You will probably need to rub it up with your worn emery paper each time you use it. It is also a good thing to keep your mandrel wrapped in greaseproof paper.

All tools should be laid out handy before you settle down to work. There is nothing worse than having to search around in a drawer or a box for a tool that you want. The tool you need should be right there beside your pad just when you want it.

### COSTS:

Sterling silver wire, 16 gauge, round, 50 cents a ft.; 20 gauge, square, 22c; round, 17c. Sterling silver sheet, 20 gauge, 42c a square in.; 22 gauge, 33c; 26 gauge, 22. Iron binding wire, 12 ft. for 5c.

Tools: Burnisher, $1.68; chisel, $\frac{3}{8}$ in., 40c; draw plates, various shapes, $7.25 to $8.15; drawing tonges, $4.40; soldering tweezers, 60c; doming block, $3.85; doming punches, various sizes, 38c to 80c; engraving tools, 75c to $2.40 each; handles, 26c; ring mandrel, $2.75; mallet, wooden, 93c; rawhide, $1.25; hand drill, $4.20; set of drill points, 50c; ring gauge sets, $1.48; ring buffs, 1 in. 32c, 3 in. 88c.

These prices were current at the end of 1966. They are subject to fluctuation and are given only as a guide. They are not binding on any jewellers' supplier.

# 9

## THINGS TO MAKE

### by Laurel Gorn

The easiest things for a beginner to make are pieces in metal alone and these will give experience in the techniques of beating and chasing. A fish shape that can be worn either as a brooch or a pendant is simple and yet can be made interesting by texturing.

First cut out a fish shape about 2½ x 2 in. with fins and tail in stiff paper. Mark a circle for an eye and cut this out leaving a fairly large round hole. Paste this down on a piece of 24 gauge sterling silver sheet and saw round the paper shape. Scratch a circle around the hole.

Wash the paper off the metal, anneal and pickle. Take a doming punch, lay the shape over a piece of lino or a lead block and punch hard on the scratched circle. This will raise a dome on the underside of the fish. Turn metal over and this will now be the front side of the fish.

If you possess a ring punch such as those used by carpenters (it can be bought from a hardware store for a few cents) place this over the dome, hit it sharply with the hammer and this will leave a deep ring round the dome. Otherwise you can take a pointed tool—a nail will do— and punch little indents close together all round the dome.

Turn the fish over again and with a small dome punch, or the rounded head of a nail, punch all over the body of the fish, being careful to avoid the big eye dome. This will create a scale effect on the front of the fish and also give it a rounded surface. Do not use the punch on the fins and tail.

When the back of the fish has been punched all over, turn it front side up again. If it is now a bit out of shape, put it right gently with the wooden mallet, but don't flatten it. By this time the metal will need annealing and pickling again.

Using the flat of the hammer, straighten the fins and tail. Now take a chisel punch and with the fish still front side 'up, mark deep lines on the fins and tail, fanning out from the body. Finally, to give life to the eye, make a dent slightly off centre. The eye may then need doming up again from the back, but the small dent will remain (see sketch Page 126).

So far it has not been necessary to do any soldering, but before you can hang the piece on a chain you will have to solder a thin strip of metal at the back of the top fin. Cut this strip about ¾ in. x ⅛ in. Flux one end of it and flux the back of the fish just below the top of the fin. Solder on the end of the strip, playing the torch flame over the whole piece until the solder melts.

Drop the piece into the pickle, then brush it well under the running tap with the brass brush. Look it over for scratches and rough places with the file and emery paper. Polish with tripoli, immerse in liver of sulphur solution until it turns black, then rub well with rouge paste to bring up the highlights.

Round the free end of the soldered strip with the file, then bend this end over with the round-nosed pliers until it meets the soldered end. Turn the tip outwards a little until it looks like a shepherd's crook, press the end down to the metal and the fish is ready to go on a silver chain. The strip loop at the back should not show from the front.

## CONTRASTING STYLES OF BROOCHES

Now try an appliqued free-form piece. Cut any shape that takes your fancy from 24 gauge sheet then cut another smaller shape. Anneal and pickle the smaller piece and beat it all over with the ball end of your hammer. It will bend into a concave shape so turn it over and beat it with the wooden mallet. You may have to anneal it again first.

The beaten piece is now sweat-soldered to the larger piece that you left plain. Flux all over the back of the beaten piece and place flat pieces of solder round the edge of it. Melt this solder with your torch, pickle and rinse.

Reflux the soldered back of the piece and lay this on the side of the plain piece that you have now fluxed. Arrange the beaten piece in a position that looks balanced and yet is not exactly in the middle. It can overlap in places. Now play the flame over the whole piece until you see the top piece settle with a shimmer of solder around the edges. Pickle and rinse after the red heat fades.

Either drill or punch a small hole in one side of the piece, through both thicknesses of metal if you like. Thread one end of the piercing saw blade through the hole and saw a small piece out. Take a short piece of 16 or 18 gauge round wire, curl one end and hammer the other end flat.

Pass the flattened end through the hole and solder it to the back of the piece.

The soldering heat will anneal both plate and wire so that you will be able to hammer the curled end of the wire hard down against the sheet with your wooden mallet. Flux along the wire and solder it to the sheet. You may also like to decorate the piece with one or two small silver balls.

To complete the brooch, you have to solder a pin joint and catch on the back. Although sterling silver pin joints and catches can be made, they are usually bought from a jewellers' supply shop.

Sterling silver wire is too soft for brooch pins. Silver-plated pins can be bought, but these must not be attached until all the soldering has been done or the plating will burn off and the pin become soft. But the best pins are made from nickel silver wire, either in 18 or 20 gauge according to the weight of the brooch for which you want it.

Soldering the joint and catch requires a little care. The joint will stand up by itself, but the safety catch must be held with tweezers and dropped on the solder as soon as it melts; or a better way I find is to clamp the catch in a bobby-pin which will keep it in place for soldering.

Keep the torch flame well away from little findings such as joints and catches or the solder will run to them and not on the brooch itself. If the flame is kept on the brooch, the findings heat at the same rate and a good join is made when the solder melts.

After soldering both findings and before cutting your pin wire, make a tiny circle in the end of the wire and fit it into the joint. This gives you the exact length of the pin. Cut it so that only about one-sixteenth of an inch will protrude from the safety catch. Remove the pin, sharpen the end to a long point and emery it well.

With most joints you will find the 20 gauge wire is too loose a fit to mount your pin and you will have to use 18 gauge filed down slightly. Push it through both holes in the sides of the joint and the loop in your pin until about an eighth of an inch protrudes through.

Bend this protruding wire sharply over with the flat-nosed pliers and, while holding it firmly, also bend the other end of the wire round and squeeze both ends together. Snip off the wire as close as you can and carefully file it down until it is almost level with the side of the joint.

By this time you will have learned a good deal about your tools and materials and what can be expected from them. You should also have gained control of your blowtorch and an understanding of soldering techniques.

Flower and leaf shapes are used a good deal in jewellery-making. Sprays can be made and jewels set in flower centres.

Having learned to tool the metal with hammer and punches, try making a simple rose. From a round disc of 24 gauge sheet about an inch in diameter, cut five small vee shapes at equal distances around the edge. Already these will begin to look like petals.

With a file round out between the vees. Anneal the piece, then take a ball punch and hollow each petal, keeping the centre of the flower flat.

Cut out a smaller disc and shape the petals in a similar way, anneal and with a centre punch or the point of a nail, punch little indents close together in the centre.

Turn the piece over and with a chisel punch make deep lines from each vee to the edge of the punched centre. These lines will mark the petals. Punch hollows in each petal as you did with the larger piece.

Both pieces should now be buttercup-shaped. Sweat solder the smaller piece into the centre of the larger and you should have a wild rose with a double row of petals.

Flat one end of a piece of 18 or 16 gauge round wire and solder this to the back of the rose as a stalk. Make another rose and cut out three leaf shapes, a little smaller than the roses. Anneal these leaves, punch veins down the centre of each leaf with smaller veins branching from them.

Before soldering these leaves to the rose stalks, try out your spray by arranging roses and leaves in different ways until you hit on a design you like. Finally both roses can be joined together by winding a twist of wire around both stalks and soldering this in place.

Attaching the brooch findings will take a little planning and perhaps require little flats to be filed on the back of the piece to take the pin joint and catch. Let this brooch be a reminder to study nature and learn to interpret different flowers and leaves in metal.

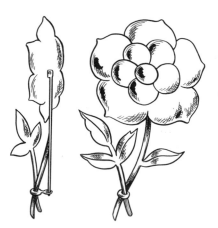

*This rose chased and domed in sterling silver makes an attractive brooch when fitted with a pin of nickel silver.*

## MAKING A FRIENDSHIP RING

In making a friendship ring, first determine your ring size, which is then marked on the mandrel with a pencil. If you do not possess a set of ring sizes, measure round the finger with a strip of paper fairly tightly. Wrap this round the mandrel where the ends exactly meet and mark the spot.

Then lay the strip of paper down on your 24 gauge sterling silver sheet, mark the length and scribe the width you want with the dividers. Cut this piece out, anneal it and tap it with a hammer until it is perfectly flat.

Next cut two lengths of 20 gauge square wire exactly the same length as the strip of sheet silver. These must also be annealed and tapped with the hammer until they are perfectly straight.

It is almost impossible to solder both these pieces of wire to the strip at the same time. Flux and solder each in turn. You will notice that square wire takes quite a lot of heating before the solder melts.

As the wires must be very securely soldered before the ring is shaped around the mandrel, as soon as both lengths are attached, turn the piece upside down so that the square wire is flat on the steel block and tap along each side with the hammer to settle both lengths well down. Then flux both sides, play heat on the whole thing and watch to see the solder run. This makes certain that there are no unsoldered gaps on either length of wire.

Now you are ready to shape up the ring on the mandrel. Do not try to shape it around the pencil mark which is your ring size, but bend the plate around the mandrel well above this mark until the ends meet. You may have to use your hammer carefully on the ends to fit them well around.

Slide the ring down until it reaches the pencil mark on the thicker part of the mandrel. If it slips past the mark it must be too big and you will have to saw a piece off one end. If it will not reach the mark, it is too

*Stages in making a friendship ring. First, sterling silver plate and square wire soldered together is bent into a circlet over a ring mandrel. Then leaves and wire ornaments are soldered in place.*

small but that is nothing to worry about at this stage. Concentrate on filing the ends to make a good join. They should be mitred slightly so that there is no gap at all to disclose the join.

When you are satisfied that the join is very close-fitting, place the ring join downwards on your asbestos pad, flux and solder, remembering to play the heat opposite the join at first. By now the ring is likely to be a little out of shape. While it is still soft after soldering, place it over the mandrel and tap it gently.

If the ring is too small to reach the pencil mark, continue tapping it with the rawhide or wooden mallet and it will stretch a little. It should gradually reach the mark without too much trouble. If it is too big all you can do is cut a piece out and file the join up carefully again.

When you are sure the ring is a perfect circlet and the correct size, you can start to make small twist wire sections. This is not easy. Instead of cutting the twist wire to make the first join, file one end of it flat and solder that small piece to the plate alongside the square wire.

Once this is well joined, zig-zag the twist wire around the ring until you know the length you need. Only then can you cut it off. Each zig-zag is soldered where it touches the square wire. When you come to the end, make a good close join with the start of the wire and solder down.

Make small leaves in the manner described in the previous chapter. Four to six will be needed depending on the size of the ring and each is sweat soldered after being shaped up. Each leaf is then refluxed, the ring is fluxed and leaves placed across the twist wire to appear as if growing from it like leaves on a vine. Small scrolls or curls of twist wire are fitted between the leaves.

These scrolls must be rubbed flat on one side with emery paper and sweat soldered. Finally leaves and scrolls are secured in place. The ring is then cleaned up with file and emery and polished either by hand or machine.

## MAKING A FILIGREE BRACELET

A popular type of bracelet is based on filigree of flattened coils of fine wire in forms of 18 or 20 gauge square wire. Most linked bracelets are 6½ to 7 in. in diameter.

To arrive at the number of forms and their dimensions, mark this length on a piece of paper and divide it, say, into five equal parts. Width is a matter of choice but your first one should be kept fairly narrow— not more than one inch wide—as there is a lot of work to be done.

The best method is to first make a form with copper wire. This will determine the length of wire needed for each section. Straighten out this

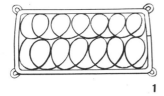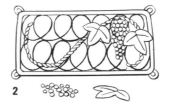

*A section of a bracelet or necklet is fashioned from square wire and filled in with filigree. Then ornaments of twist wire, leaves and tiny silver grapes are soldered to the filigree.*

copper wire and use it as a pattern for five equal lengths of silver wire. Anneal each of these and then they can be either shaped to the diagram on your paper or joined in circlets and shaped with flat-nosed pliers.

All five sections are shaped and matched as closely as possible. The joins of the wire should be kept at the short ends. The flattened coil is then cut in pieces to fit in rows across the square wire sections and soldered in place.

The filigree is then used as a backing on which a vine design can be built up with twisted wire, small leaves and tiny silver balls soldered to represent bunches of grapes. Finally the sections are joined with links of 20 gauge square wire, two for each section. Alternative designs can be cut from 24 gauge sheet for each of the bracelet sections, punched or chased and sweat soldered to the filigree.

A box snap is the best type of catch for this bracelet and is not difficult to make. Cut a small oblong in 24 gauge plate about ¾ in. x ½ in. With the dividers score a line less than an eighth of an inch from the edge on three sides. Cut out the little squares marked in the two end corners with the snips.

Anneal the piece, then carefully bend the two marked sides until they are at right angles with the flat-nosed pliers until the two corners meet. Mark the angles as sharply as possible. Anneal again if necessary. Now cut out another oblong slightly longer than the box-shaped piece you have just formed and sweat solder it to the edges of the box with the extra length protruding at the open end.

File out a square slot in the centre of this protruding piece, filing it back to the edge of the box. Turn up the remaining ends of the protruding piece until they fit against the box. These ends should reach half-way up the width of the box, leaving a slit for the tongue to slip through. Solder them firmly.

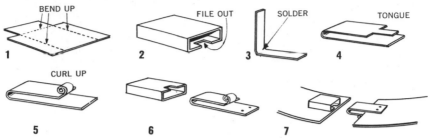

*Stages in making a box clasp for a bracelet.*

Cut a strip of metal three times as long as the box and as wide as the inside of it. Bend this sharply into the form of a vee and prop it between two pieces of scrap asbestos or a bobby-pin. Flux the apex of the vee and melt a fragment of solder in it. This is to strengthen this section.

Bend the two sides of the vee flat together and hammer the bend well. Without the solder it would break in half. This forms the tongue of your snap. You will find that hammering has widened your piece a little so that you will have to file it to fit into the slot of your box.

Round the sharp corners and file them smooth. Try the tongue in the box and, if tight, adjust it with the file and emery paper until you can slide it in and out with ease. Push it right into the box and mark the tongue where the end protrudes and also with the width of the slot in the box.

The protruding part of the tongue is cut away at each side leaving a strip in the centre that is the width of the slot. The part of the tongue which fits into the box should be adjusted so that when it is pushed into the box, the narrow strip at the end snaps up into the slot and holds fast.

Finally the box of the catch is sweat soldered to the underside of one section of the bracelet. The end of the tongue must be drilled with small holes to take the two round links by which it is attached to the opposite end section.

## A PAIR OF LEAF EARRINGS

Earrings, though simple to make, must be very neat because they are small. They should never look clumsy or out of balance. This pair have a leaf design as the base.

Cut a leaf shape about an inch long in stiff paper. Make this leaf so that its pointed end curls around a little. This forms a pattern from which can be cut two shapes in a fine gauge silver sheet. Tool these slightly with a chisel punch to form veins down the centre of each.

*Leaf-shaped earrings chased and jewelled with cabochons. Screw findings are soldered in place on the back of each leaf but not bent into shape until polishing is complete.*

To set a stone on these leaves only outer bezels are needed. Carefully measure your matched cabochons, cut the bezel for each and fit them exactly. Solder the ends and try the stones for height. If they are too high, file the bezels down a little. Rub down the underside of each on emery paper to make sure they are absolutely level.

Both earrings should have been cut exactly alike, but after annealing and before punching be careful to place them as they will be worn, opposite to each other. They should curve towards each other, not having the curve of the leaf on each going the same way.

Bear this in mind when you place the bezels in position on the base of each leaf. Flux all around the undersides of both and place little pieces of solder inside each bezel. Solder placed on the outside is likely to spread over the leaf as it melts. Bring the flame down very carefully as it is very easy for the little bits of solder to be misplaced and fail to secure the bezel.

When the bezels are in place all that remains to be done is to attach the screws or clips to the back. Sterling silver earring screws can be bought from most jewellers' suppliers. Don't get plated screws as the plating will burn off during soldering. The best type to buy are straight and are not bent up into the normal screw shape until polishing is finished. They are easier to polish while straight. All you need to do is to place the little rounded ends of these screws about the centre of the back of each leaf and solder securely in place.

Faceted stones can also be used for this type of earring but in that case a collet will be needed which will allow light to get through and this collet must then be soldered to the leaf. If that is not feasible, make the collet and build a pattern around it with wire or a piece of plate.

Clear or opaque stones in lentil shapes which have a curve on either side of the stone can be made into drop earrings, although it is not an easy task and requires considerable practice to make a success of it.

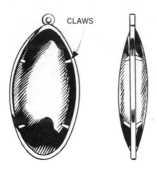

*A collet with claws to hold a lentil cabochon. This device can be used for either a pendant, brooch or ear-drops.*

A thin strip of metal is fitted around the edge of the stone. Wire claws are soldered to this strip with the same length of claw on either side and a small ring soldered on top. The claws are pressed on either side of the stone to set it. It is then attached to the earring screw by another small ring.

## MAKING A TIE SLIDE

A tie slide is a useful item of men's jewellery which is very simple to make. Cut a strip of 22 gauge sterling silver sheet, about three inches long by a quarter to half-an-inch wide, according to the width you prefer.

Before annealing this strip mark the half-way on it and about an eighth of an inch from this mark, drill a small hole through which you can thread the blade of your piercing saw. Very carefully saw out a strip of metal, about a sixteenth of an inch from the edges of the strip to within a quarter of an inch of the end. This smaller strip should be about an inch long with one end still attached to the piece.

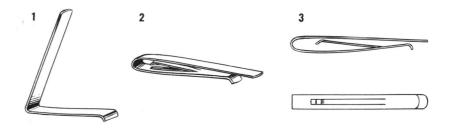

*How a strip of silver is shaped into a tie-clip. The third picture shows the clip from the side and also from below, illustrating how a spring is cut in the lower half of the clip.*

This strip is carefully pulled out a little and the end bent down until it fits into the slot from which the strip was cut. This forms the spring that will hold the slide in position. Do not anneal the piece or the metal will lose its elasticity.

Taking the piece in your round-nosed pliers bend it double until the two ends meet. Do not allow it to go too flat. There must be a decided curve in the bend. The spring should now be on the inside with the bent end touching the underside of what is now the front of your slide so that it will grip the tie firmly.

If you want to solder a bezel on to the strip, this must be done before it is bent. Make the bezel to fit the stone in the usual way. An inner bezel is not needed as the strip of metal will hold the stone in place. Alternatively you could solder a pattern in wire or tiny silver balls to relieve the plainness of the piece.

Soldering will soften the metal of course and it will have to be tapped with a hammer on the steel block to restore its hardness. Bend it over carefully and if it is still too soft, tap it again gently but don't flatten it too much. When the hardness has been restored, you will find you have quite a strong spring.

## MAKING A FANCY SPOON

First step in making a fancy spoon is cutting out the shape of the bowl in 22 gauge sheet. Spoons are normally oval in shape or perhaps egg-shaped, so just cut out the shape which you like best.

After being annealed the metal can either be beaten into a lead block when it will shape up of its own accord or you can first beat a hollow into the lead block with your hammer, shaping it to the size you want, and then beat the piece of sheet into this hollow with a rounded wooden punch.

A little adjustment will be needed to keep the bowl in good shape. One way of doing this is to place it upside down on a steel block, place a piece of lino or felt over it and tap over the lino with your hammer. Run a file over the edges of the bowl to give them an even appearance.

An easy spoon handle is made from 12 gauge round wire. You will need a piece about four inches long. This should be flattened a little, slightly more at the top of the handle than at the part which is to be attached to the bowl so as to give a tapered appearance.

It depends on the way in which you wish to decorate the top of the handle. If you decide on a small flower, you will have to flatten the top a little more to solder the flower down. Complete the handle before attaching the spoon bowl to it. The bowl should be the last thing to be soldered.

Having soldered your flower shape down on the top of the handle, take a piece of 18 gauge wire, flat one end, and solder this on the underside of the flower close up to the centre and touching where the flattened end of the handle is soldered. Twist this around the handle like a vine for about an inch and a half.

Small leaves can be cut, veined and domed up and sweat soldered on this stalk. You may need four or five small leaves to give a realistic appearance to the flower.

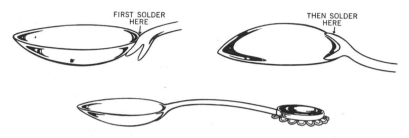

*Soldering a spoon bowl to the handle is best done in two stages—first with the bowl upwards and then downwards after the claw end of the handle has been snugly fitted in place. A cabochon set in a filigree bezel looks well on the handle of a fancy sugar-spoon.*

Before soldering on the handle, the end which goes under the bowl must be hammered very flat. Sometimes this only needs to be rounded off with a file and the solder sweated on to it, but a claw effect is popular. For this two saw cuts are made up into the flat piece for about a quarter of an inch. This will give three claws. Spread the outside ones, sharpen them to a point and curve them outwards a little.

Attaching the bowl to the handle is one of the trickiest parts. Before doing this, make a slight step with your knife-edge file at the end of the handle just above the claws. The best way, I think, to hold the spoon in position for soldering is with a bobby pin.

Make a little stand with the pin for the spoon to rest against. Push the handle up close to this little stand and rest the edge of the bowl in the step and lean it against the pin. This will hold it quite firmly.

Flux the underside of the bowl and the step in the handle, seat the bowl in it and lay a small piece of solder against the join. Keep the torch flame mainly on the handle as this is the heaviest part, then move the flame up and down the whole piece until you see the solder melt.

At this stage the bowl is only partly attached to the handle. Having pickled and cleaned it, put it over a piece of domed metal or a thickish domed piece of wood such as the rounded end of a broomstick. See that the dome fits into the bowl and then tap the claws down until they are snugly fitted against the rounded side of the bowl.

Now lay the spoon, bowl down, over a small piece of asbestos. Flux around the claws, lay solder against them and play the heat as before until the solder runs.

As yet the spoon is not likely to be quite the shape you want because the handle will stand up too high. Take the handle very firmly with the flat-nosed pliers well up against the bowl and bend it down a little.

This will complete your spoon. Brush it up with the brass brush under a running tap. Spoons need a lot of cleaning up because they must be polished well. Spend a lot of time with the file and emery paper, especially on the inside of the bowl.

To avoid burns the bowl must be dipped in a hot and strong solution of boracic acid. This leaves a white coating over the metal which protects it from burn marks. Dip the bowl in the solution each time before applying heat. It will also give the silver a much brighter appearance.

You may like to set a gemstone in the handle of your spoon. The best and strongest way to do this is to attach a shaped piece of sheet silver to the top of the handle on which you can then solder a bezel to fit your cabochon. No inner bezel is needed. A piece of twisted wire can be soldered around the bezel to finish it off.

## MAKING A BUTTERKNIFE

A simple butterknife can be made of 20 gauge sterling silver sheet and 14 gauge round wire. Cut a strip of sheet about 2 in. by half-an-inch. About 6 in. of the wire will be needed for the handle.

Anneal both wire and plate. Then hammer your two-inch strip of plate into a blade on the steel block. Hammer hard until you get a knife edge on it. You will find the blade will take a slight curve which adds to the design. Be careful not to beat the curved top edge of the knife.

When you have made it as flat and even as you can, your blade will show beat marks. If you prefer the appearance of a beaten blade continue beating carefully until the marks are even. If you want a smooth blade, file the blade over until all the marks have disappeared.

Now take your length of 14 gauge wire and bend it into the long shape of a knife handle. This can form a rhythmic pattern by following the curve of the back of the blade. Bend the wire fairly closely so that the

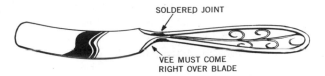

*How the butterknife is made from silver plate and heavy gauge wire.*

two ends touch, then curl one of the ends away, forming a slight vee-shape. Solder the two sides that touch together, leaving the vee.

Lightly flatten the whole of the wire with the hammer. You will now have a long loop form and if you lay this down with the vee end on the curved side of the blade, you will see that the curve can follow through right along the handle.

Now decide on the design you are going to fit into the loop of the handle. Flatten as much 18 gauge wire as you require and make scrolls and twists. Fit these inside the loop until you have made a kind of filigree design.

When all this is soldered in place turn your attention to the vee end. The ends of wire which form the vee must be filed down to a point working entirely from inside the vee. Then file the points down until they are level with your knife blade.

Put the vee in position. It should overlap the blade by at least a quarter of an inch. Sweat solder the vee ends to the blade. Of course this blade is still just a curved strip of the plate which does not look much like a knife. Use your saw to cut the blade into a shape similar to that shown in the sketch.

If you want to set a gemstone in the handle, this must be taken into consideration before the wire is bent. Make the bezel first and fit the stone into it temporarily. Place the bezel inside the loop as you bend the wire to obtain a snug fit. Keep the stone in the bezel while you are doing this or it will otherwise be pushed out of shape.

As soon as you have fitted the bezel, take out the stone, flux between the bezel and the wire loop and solder it in position. If you feel your cabochon is not sufficient decoration, you can fill the remaining space in the handle with filigree in flattened 18 gauge wire.

After soldering is completed, all edges must be trued up. The edge of the blade will have to be smoothed around and bevelled a little on either side. Emery the whole piece well and use a file where necessary, particularly to remove the sharp edges where the handle is soldered to the blade.

The blade will burn very easily and should be protected by dipping in hot boracic acid solution before being heated.

## COSTS:

Prices current at the end of 1966 were: Sterling silver 12 gauge round wire, $1.30 a foot 14 gauge round, 78 cents; 14 gauge square, $1.07; 18 gauge round, 28c; 18 gauge square, 38c; 20 gauge square, 22c; 20 gauge sterling silver sheet, 42c a square inch; 22 gauge, 33c; 24 gauge, 27c. Standard amounts are a little cheaper.

Sterling silver joints, 3c each; safety catches, 12c; with bases, 20c; jump rings, 12c to 36c a dozen; ear screws, 32c a pair. Nickel silver brooch pin wire, 4 ft. for 12c.

These prices are subject to fluctuation and they are not binding on any jeweller's supplier.

# 10

# ELEMENTARY ENAMELLING

## by Laurel Gorn

SIMPLE ENAMELLING CAN BE DONE with very little equipment, and with enamels readily available at present, every jeweller should be able to add this process to his or her repertoire.

For small pieces, if you have a propane gas torch, all you will need in equipment will be a tripod or large fruit tin and a piece of wire mesh. I find the fruit tin best as it helps to keep the heat in. Cut a square hole in the side of the tin and a large round hole in the top of it. Stand the tin on an asbestos sheet on the table, place the iron mesh over the hole in the top and you are ready to go.

Enamels are obtained in small jars in powder form or in fine sticks and beads or balls. If enamels are to be kept any length of time, it is best to buy them in frit form if you can. This is slab enamel broken into rough pieces and they are pulverised in a mortar with a pestle and a little water. Occasionally, the water must be drained off and fresh water added before the process is completed.

It is best for the beginner to get a few powdered colours in small jars. Enamels come in opaque and transparent form and there is also an opalised enamel.

For first attempts, copper is the best metal to use. Cut a simple shape not bigger than $2\frac{1}{2}$ in. in 18 gauge copper. Clean this in pickle, rinse and scrub with powdered kitchen cleanser and steel wool. Drop it into clean water and if no bubbles form on the metal, you will know it is free of grease. This is important as enamel will not take over grease.

After cleaning do not handle with the fingers but pick up with tweezers and dry in a paper tissue. If the metal is very dirty, heat it before dropping in pickle. Keep the clean piece wrapped in tissue until ready to be enamelled.

Before using the enamels they must be washed. For the opaques one washing will do. Empty the jar into a small bowl (not metal) and cover with clean water. Stir with a spoon or stick, then drain the liquid off into another bowl. The transparents will need several washings until the water is no longer milky.

Do not throw out the drained-off water but let it stand overnight and when the clean liquid is poured away, there will be a thick sediment in the bottom of the bowl. Keep this for counter-enamelling later. Counter-enamelling is the term used for enamelling the back of the piece.

The washed enamel can be dried in a shallow pan over a hotplate, but don't let it get too hot and keep stirring it until it is quite dry. Then it can be put back in its original jar.

Start with an opaque enamel, select a colour, remove the lid from the jar and place over the neck two thicknesses of old nylon stocking and secure it with a rubber band. Place the clean copper piece over a sheet of paper or dry tissue and dust the enamel evenly over it until all the metal is well covered.

Carefully lift the piece with a spatula or broad knife on to the iron mesh in the centre of the hole in your tin. Light your gas jet, push it through the hole in the side of the tin until the tip of the flame is under the copper piece. You will need the full jet.

You will find it fascinating to watch the enamel change texture, first turning pebbly, then shiny and smooth and red hot. When it is quite smooth, remove the heat and leave the piece where it is until cool. You will see it gradually restored to its original colour as it cools.

A second colour can be placed on this or a series of colours in the form of a design and the piece placed on the mesh and the enamel melted as before.

The enamels can also be used wet and must be laid on with a small spatula. This can be made from a short piece of wire of about 16 gauge flattened at one end. The other end can be stuck into a handle. Sometimes the wet enamel refuses to drop off the spatula and a pointer is needed to push it off. This is simply a sharpened piece of the same wire.

The wet enamel is spread over the piece with the spatula not more than one thirty-second of an inch thick. Smooth it well and place the piece on the mesh over the hole in the tin. Heat very gently at first until the enamel dries.

You could try a little cloisonne. Solder a fine wire design, either in copper or silver on to the copper plate, using very little solder. Clean the piece well as before, then using the wet inlay method, carefully fill in the empty spaces between the wires. Different colours can be used.

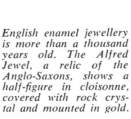

*A simple design in Cloisonne enamelling. Enamels of different colours are fused in the various sections or cloisonnes, which are divided by strips of flat wire.*

*English enamel jewellery is more than a thousand years old. The Alfred Jewel, a relic of the Anglo-Saxons, shows a half-figure in cloisonne, covered with rock crystal and mounted in gold.*

When the piece is fired, it should be stoned down with a fine silicon carbide stone under a running tap until the wires are level with the enamel. Then the piece is fired again to restore the shine.

When you have tried out the opaques, turn to the transparents. First dust on the clean piece a clear flux that is like clear glass when fired. When the piece is cool, dust over the flux any transparent colour and fire again.

Before doing any serious work, sample pieces about an inch square should be made; a square for each colour. These are invaluable when working out colour designs.

The greatest number of experiments should be tried with the transparents. Try colours over the metal and over the flux, try the transparents in the same way over scraps of silver and compare them with the same colours over copper.

Enamels can be used over sterling silver with success but care must be taken not to melt the silver. Fine silver with its higher melting point is safer, but as it is also softer than sterling, get it in heavy gauge—not less than 16 gauge—or it will warp and the enamel will crack.

Enamelling silver is more complicated than enamelling copper as the enamel tends to shrink away from the sides on silver and nearly always must be fired a second or even a third time. The enamel should be pushed well out to the edges if laid on wet.

With all enamelling, it is better to shape the metal slightly as it is not so likely to warp as on the flat. Anneal the metal and beat with the ball end of the hammer on a steel block, not a lead block, until it is domed a little. Clean up well and the enamel can be used either on the concave or convex side of the metal. Under transparents, the beat marks enhance the appearance.

When making jewellery all soldering, putting on findings and so on, must be done before enamelling and the findings protected with a coating of yellow ochre made into a paste. This will dry hard during heating but will wash off under water. The piece can be polished by the methods described in Chapter Seven.

As you progress you will want to know more about techniques and methods. You may consider the expense of a kiln but in the meantime it will be interesting to find out just what can be done with the blowtorch.

At the present time kilns are not easy to obtain and are expensive. A very good kiln costing somewhere round $80 is a dental kiln which will take a piece of up to say 4 in. and small things such as, say, ashtrays can be enamelled successfully in these. Also in a kiln pieces can be counter-enamelled which adds to their attraction and their strength.

At the moment smaller kilns are at the stage of development and testing and should shortly be on the market. The larger the kiln, of course, the more expensive it is and the more expensive it will be to run. But if any serious work is contemplated in the future, provision should be made for running a kiln.

In France during the Renaissance, the Limoges or grisaille techniques were highly developed. The enamels, pulverised to a very fine powder, were mixed with a light oil and painted on an already enamelled surface. A simple form of this technique can be used on your small pieces.

Cloisonne and plique-au-jour became favourite techniques of the Chinese and later the Japanese. Champleve and basse-taille were brought to perfection by Byzantine artists.

Plique-au-jour or window enamelling is the technique of enamelling over pierced metal or close wire work. The prepared piece is laid on a mica sheet and the cells filled with transparent enamel and fired. Several applications of enamel are needed to fill the cells and the result is striking when the light shows through. This is most suitable for drop earrings.

In basse-taille work, the metal is chased and the enamel may cover the whole surface, being deeper in the chased sections, or may simply fill in the chased parts, leaving the rest of the metal showing. In champleve work the metal is deeply carved or gouged and the enamel brought level with the surface metal or the metal can be deeply etched. In all these techniques the enamels are inlaid wet.

Niello is another form of enamels developed in the East and much used there today. It is a mixture of non-ferrous metals and sulphur inlaid into a grooved design and fires black. There are several formulas for making niello and some of these have the advantage of being applied successfully to metals of low melting point.

Enamelling has infinite possibilities and the modern versions have been brought to a high state of perfection in Denmark and the United States of America. Small pieces fired with the blowtorch are not difficult and can be really beautiful in the hands of an expert, but kiln enamelling has many pitfalls.

Enamels fire at different temperatures. Most reds and oranges especially opaques, burn out in too hot a kiln, so they should be added in the last firing. In most colours, blacks, whites and fluxes, there are soft, medium and hard types. The first firing should be a hard enamel and the last a soft one. The enamels are numbered on the jars and usually indicate the type of hardness.

You will now understand that a great deal of experiment and experience is required before any kiln work is attempted. The more small labelled samples you make, the better will be your work later, as these will be of great assistance when designing your piece. Label the samples with colour numbers, type of hardness, whether over flux or whether the colour is directly applied to the metal.

Enamels appear at their best over silver and gold; cool colours over silver and warm over gold. Transparent reds, oranges and yellows look rich and very beautiful over gold and blues over silver.

Transparent colours look well over a ground coat of white opaque. Use a hard or medium white; soft, in successive firings, will show greenish patches. These often tone in with the design, but if you don't want this effect, use the hard whites and creams when colours are to be fired over them, especially the transparents. Black can also be difficult, burning out with successive firings.

At all times cleanliness is essential. When using the dusting method of applying enamels, see that the paper under the piece is quite clean, so that any excess enamel can be poured back into the jar and used again.

Sometimes when the iron mesh over the tin gets red hot, a fire scale forms on it and specks of this can fly off and land on the melted enamel.

To avoid this, rub the mesh with a yellow ochre paste which will prevent the fire scale forming.

It is best to get a Nichrome or stainless steel mesh if you can. Iron fly wire gauze can be used if nothing else is available but it needs renewing from time to time.

## COSTS:

Copper sheet is available in gauges from 24 to 16 at 18 cents to 50 cents respectively for a four-inch square and 65 cents to $1.70 for a 12 x 6 in. rectangle. Corresponding prices apply to pieces between these sizes. A 20 in. length of copper solder costs about 22 cents and a ¼ lb. tin of flux costs $1.20.

Six-inch squares of steel wire mesh cost 22 cents; stainless steel, 72 cents. High temperature grade 12 gauge nickel chrome wire for swirling sticks and tripods costs 19 cents a ft.

Enamels—1 oz. bottles of Group 1 powder colours and flux cost 35 cents each; Group 2 colours, 45 cents; 50 gram packets of Group 1 ball colours, $2.35 each; Group 2 colours, $3; seven-inch phials of Group 1 thread colours, $1.35; Group 2 colours, $1.95. Glitter enamel powder costs $1.50 an oz. and gum tragacanth, a solution of which is applied to metals before dusting with enamel, costs 35 cents a bottle.

These were ruling prices at the end of 1966, and are subject to fluctuation. They are not binding on any jewellers' suppliers.

## PEARL JEWELLERY

Among the gems that are not stones is the pearl, produced in the shells of certain oysters, abalones and fresh-water mussels. Pearls are fished in all the warmer seas, including northern Australia, the finest coming from the Persian Gulf. Fresh-water pearls are gathered from lakes and rivers in Europe, Asia and the United States.

A pearl grows as the result of an irritant, such as a grain of sand, becoming lodged under the tissue lining the oyster's shell. The oyster protects itself by coating the irritant particle with successive layers of nacre and aragonite. Movements of the tissue roll the growing pearl into a spherical shape.

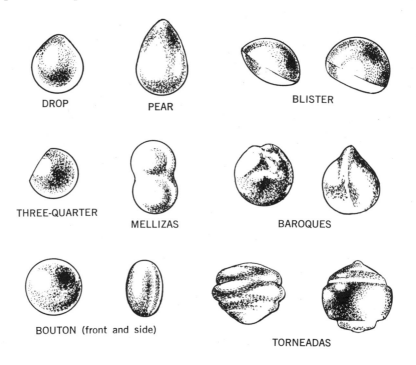

DROP          PEAR                    BLISTER

THREE-QUARTER
              MELLIZAS          BAROQUES

BOUTON (front and side)
                        TORNEADAS

Most of the world's pearls are now grown in Japan on what are literally pearl farms. In 1893 a 35-year-old Japanese named Kokichi Mikimoto crowned five years of effort by growing cultured pearls. These were half or blister pearls, completely round pearls not being produced until 1905. Meanwhile the dreaded red tide of plankton had twice destroyed most of Mikimoto's oysters.

Long before his death in 1954 at the age of 96, Mikimoto had established a great industry. His method was to insert a mother-of-pearl pellet into the tissue of the oyster which was then placed in a wire-mesh cage and allowed to grow in the sea for three to five years.

The resulting pearls match the finest of natural pearls in shape, colour and lustre. Most are spheres but some are misshapen as baroques, torneadas, twins (mellizas) and blister pearls. The most prized pearls are almost white or pink, but other natural tints include yellow, green, blue, lavender, caramel and black.

The price of pearls is determined by their size, quality, shape and colour. Sizes range from two millimetres to 12 millimetres in diameter and larger size means higher price. Top quality pearls are spherical, lustrous and flawless while irregular shapes are lower in price.

In terms of cash, they range from about 20 cents for a three millimetre pearl to $8 for an 8 mm. Other sizes: 4 mm., 60c; 5 mm., $1.20; 6 mm., $2.60; 7 mm., $4. A top quality 9¾ mm. pearl sells at about $160. Baroque and three-quarter pearls are cheaper.

Laurel Gorn contributes this advice on setting pearls: "Half-drill and fit over a little peg, the peg being either soldered in the centre of a shallow cup to fit the pearl or on a small flat disc. In some cases the pearl can just be attached to the peg with pearl cement or Araldite without a supporting cup or disc.

"A professional type peg can be made with two pieces of half-round wire. To make these draw through the same hole in the draw-plate two pieces of annealed 20 gauge round wire. Keep drawing these down until the two halves will fit together into the hole in the pearl.

"Drill a small hole in the bottom of the cup or disc and push the double wire through the hole. Solder into the plate, then cut off the wire, leaving just enough to fit down into the pearl.

"Before setting the pearl, open up the two half wires to make them spring a little, then apply a touch of pearl cement or Araldite to the top of the peg and hold the two halves close. Push the pearl well down over them, when they will spring slightly apart inside the pearl and hold it tightly.

"An easier peg to make is to twist 25 or 26 gauge wire tightly, insert into the hole in the cup, solder and cut off as before. The twisted wire acts like a screw and, with a touch of cement, the pearl can be screwed on to it. Naturally, all polishing on the piece must be completed before pearls are added.

"In using pearl cement, both the piece and the pearl must be warmed. The cement is melted and touched quickly to the warmed peg and the warmed pearl pushed into place. Araldite is easier to fix (a spring clothes peg makes a good clamp while it hardens) but if at any time the pearl has to be removed, it is only necessary to warm the pearl cement."

Special drills can be bought for drilling pearls. Polishing or rubbing pearls is useless, but they can be cleaned with a cloth moistened with alcohol and warm water, followed by another cloth dipped in warm water only. Avoid heat and acid for both can have disasterous effects on pearls.

Imitation pearls are produced by coating a plastic or glass core with a lacquer composed of guanine, a substance made from fish scales, nitro-cellulose and amyl acetate. However, these are not likely to be of much interest to hobby jewellery-makers.

Three other gem materials not of mineral origin are coral, amber and ivory. At present all three are more or less overlooked in Australia.

CORAL: *Corallium rubrum*, the gem coral of the Mediterranean and Japanese waters is not often seen in Australia nowadays, which is a pity because the colours—pale rose through tomato red to maroon—look fine in silver settings.

However, new interest has lately been aroused in the black coral *Antipathes abies* quite commonly found around Australian coasts. This is a relative of the Indian Ocean material known as kings' coral from the fact that native rulers had sceptres made of it and it is also the basis of the Hawaiian coral gem industry.

This coral is not largely calcite like the red coral but composed of a horny substance that can be moulded to a certain extent as well as polished. Like all coral it is produced by a small sea creature, the coral polyp, and each tree-like growth is the home of a polyp colony.

Unlike the red coral, the main growth of which seldom exceeds a foot in length and an inch in diameter, the black coral may be large and substantial. It is now being gathered by Australian skindivers, particularly on the Barrier Reef.

Coral is brittle and best worked by hand. After careful sanding, a prepolish with tripoli followed by a paste of tin oxide produces a brilliant polish. Australian coral is pitch-black and lustrous but so far it has not been found possible to bring up the pattern of white growth rings to the same effect as in the best Hawaiian gems.

AMBER: This fossil resin is a gem of northern Europe and New Zealand kauri gum does not compare with the best Baltic amber. Wartime refugees brought some fine amber jewellery to Australia but it is now rarely seen. Amber is gathered from beaches all around the Baltic, relics of prehistoric pine forests now under the sea. It is also dredged and mined.

Colours vary from creamy yellow to rich brown and rare blue and

green varieties. Often transparent fragments contain extinct insects perfectly preserved. Cloudy amber can be cleared by boiling in linseed-oil,
adding colour to which will change the colour of the amber. Heated
amber can be pressed together to form large masses for carving. It burns
with an aromatic odour and, as a consequence, has been used as incense.

Amber is soft but it also tends to chip and is best hand-worked with
files. Use at least three grades of sanding and polish with tin oxide on a
chamois pad, finishing off with jeweller's rouge.

IVORY: Elephant tusks, of which African material is the finest, are the only
true ivory although the term is also loosely applied to teeth from whales
and hippopotamuses and walrus' tusks (morse ivory). Ivory has been
carved for at least 40,000 years and used for jewellery of all kinds,
usually inlaid with gold or silver. Some of the finest work nowadays is
still done by Indian craftsmen with meagre hand tools but ivory carving
in Japan has been commercialised.

Ivory was prized next only to jade in ancient China. Canton is a
renowned centre for highly-skilled and intricate carving. Here are made
the fantastic devil's work balls, consisting of concentric spheres carved
one inside another, often as many as 20 separate balls, of which the outer
is less than five inches in diameter.

The rising cost and diminishing supply of ivory have led to the use of
substitutes, including plastics. One of the most interesting substitutes is
vegetable ivory. This is a hard, white, compact substance found in the
ripe fruits of a variety of palms growing in Central America. When
immature, these corozo or ivory nuts contain a sweet milky fluid like
coconuts, but grow thicker, harder and drier with age.

(Information on pearls and their prices was given by the Pearl Dis-
tributors Pty. Ltd., of York Street, Sydney, who supply Mikimoto pearls
to lapidary dealers among other customers.)

# 11

# DESIGN

WHENEVER YOU GET THE CHANCE have a look at the work of the leading
contemporary jewellery artist-craftsmen. A good way of doing this is to
study the excellent pictures appearing in a number of United States
publications. Whether or not the Americans lead the world as amateur
jewellers is a moot point, but they are undoubtedly among the avant-garde
of the world's jewellery designers.

For that reason, if you are able to gather a sufficiently varied number
of specimen illustrations, it is interesting to carry out the following test.
The next time you are in the company of three or four friends pass
around the pictures and ask them to nominate the items they like best—
or perhaps dislike least.

Try to keep your friends from influencing each other's choice by
making comparisons. To a certain extent the value of the result will
depend on the composition of the group. People above the age of 30 or
so are sometimes prejudiced in favour of art forms with which they are
familiar. On the other hand, some contrary urge prompts some teenagers
to choose objects whose only appeal is freakish and shocking.

However, if the test is fairly carried out, it will throw some light on
the question of what constitutes good design. Out of a score of jewellery
designs, some few—it might be only one or two or as many as half-a-
dozen—will be more popularly liked (or less disliked) than the rest.

Examine these chosen designs. They will probably be completely
different in almost every respect. One a ring, another a brooch, the third
a bracelet . . . shapes vary, materials differ, but they will share at least
one quality in common.

Harmony is perhaps the most adequate word to describe this quality.
These designs look right. They possess the essential requirements of

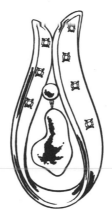

*Modern jewellery designs. The centrepiece, a band of gold and precious stones enclosing a baroque pearl, is a product of the Mikimoto artists.*

symmetry, balance and proportion. Although they may be novel and unusual, they are neither awkward nor ugly.

The quality is not confined to modern jewellery. It is found in artistic objects at every stage of human development from the ochre paintings of the cavemen to the present day. The sculptor of Queen Nefertiti knew the secret of good design more than 3,000 years ago. It has illuminated the work of artists ever since, despite the strange attempts of fashion at times to put out the light.

The harmonies of good design, presuming that popular approval qualifies certain designs to be called good, seem to be inherent in true artists, whatever their media. An appreciation of the subtleties of line, colour and texture that combine in good design are part of the artist's make-up. He has the instinct or aptitude that we call a flair.

This is not to say that being born with a flair guarantees the ability to design jewellery in the same way that being born a dog guarantees the ability to bark one day. A good deal of knowledge and experience has to be gained through study and practice on the way. The flair must be accompanied by a capacity for work and an itch for self-expression.

But it is many times more difficult for people who do not have a flair for design. Their pride and satisfaction in their work is limited and their creative efforts always seem doomed to fall short of their ambitions. The principles of design can be learned at art schools and sometimes frustrated amateur jewellers take these courses. But lectures and study are a long hard road compared to which inspiration is a short cut.

However, not everyone agrees that popularity is the proof of good design. If the production of handwrought jewellery is accepted as a fine art rather than as one of the decorative arts, the true test would be whether the work was a genuine expression of the creator's personality and talent. Whether or not it was pleasing would have very little to do with the merit of the work.

It is argued that before one can criticise or properly appreciate a production of the fine arts, one must understand the artist's outlook and what his work is trying to express. The work should be judged not by the standards of the critic, but by the standards of the artist himself.

This may be all very well for painting or music or literature, but it is an unrealistic formula to apply to jewellery unless this jewellery has been made only to be exhibited or worn by the maker. If the jewellery has been made to be worn by someone else, the standards by which it is judged are more likely to be those of the wearer than the maker. It might reasonably be expected to have been made to please the person for whom it was intended.

Jewellery made for other people to wear has to meet up to criteria of design beyond the general artistic principles of symmetry, balance and proportion. It must blend with the personality and physical appearance of the wearer.

For example, a flamboyant highly coloured woman demands jewellery of the same kind, heavy and ornate with bright colours and flashy stones . . . slave bracelets, pirate earrings, chunky rings . . . Making tiny, delicate pieces of jewellery for this Spanish-type beauty would be only a bad joke, because she would look foolish in them.

Conversely, the woman with tiny hands and small features will want bracelets and brooches, rings and earrings—especially earrings—as demure and dainty as she is herself.

Between these extremes there is plenty of scope for variety. Tall, stately women often choose formal, elegant jewellery, while some plump women prefer pendant and eardrop styles.

While stature and personality generally dictate the size, shape and mood of personal jewellery, the colour of the gemstones used depends on the hair, eyes and complexion of the wearer. Silver jewellery with pearls or waterwhite and pale-tinted gems looks best on the women with natural or artificially greyed hair. Cool greens and blues in silver settings are for the paler blondes, blues for the blue-eyed and greens for grey-eyed.

Various shades of pink and green are surprisingly effective with red hair, although this is the difficult one, ranging from copper to chestnut. Brunettes are more easily suited; rich blues and reds and greens that are

# THE ART OF ROSS FRASER

*This flower is one of the masterpieces produced by gem carver Ross Fraser of Burwood, N.S.W. The work is so delicate that it is hard to believe a gemstone yielded the beautifully marked prehnite petals or the stalks and leaves of Queensland chrysoprase. Mr. Fraser, a past president of Sydney's Western Suburbs Lapidary Club, collects his own carving materials on trips to gemfields.*

*Mr. Fraser used petals of Broken Hill rhodochrosite, green jasper leaves and stalks with a base of mottled grey chert to make this exquisite rose.*

*Below: Souvenirs of three fossicking trips combine in this attractive ornament—birds of Glen Innes smoky quartz, a bird-bath of Katoomba chert and a base of Murwillumbah petrified wood.*

*This bunch of grapes was Mr. Fraser's first gem-carving project. He sliced amethyst crystals from Broken Hill into cubes and rounded them by hand to make a three-dimensional picture, with leaves of mottled green Tasmanian serpentine and twig-thin stalks of red-brown jasper from Murwillumbah, N.S.W.*

# THE WORK OF
## A MAN IN
### HIS SEVENTIES

Joseph A. Heapy, of Waverley, N.S.W., was over 70 years of age and nearly blind in one eye when he carved the jewels shown on these pages. Below is an enlargement of the intarsia he calls Cleopatra. It is composed from gleaming opal and red obsidian on a background of Queensland opal matrix. The clothing is ornamented with inlaid gold ribbon. Actual size is 1¾ in. by 1½ in.

Some 2700 opal fragments, each one thirty-second of an inch thick, arranged between fine strands of gold form this peacock's tail. Both this magnificent inlaid gem and the butterfly below are greatly enlarged, disclosing the fantastic quality of the work.

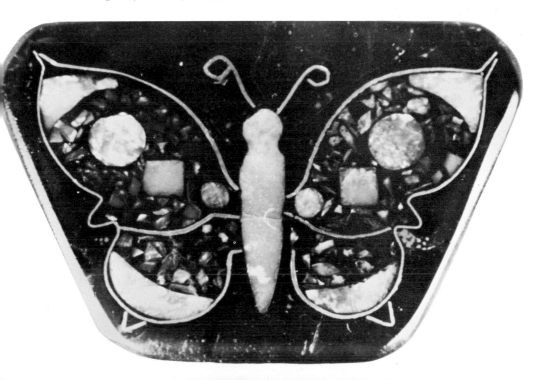

The wavy lines on a fragment of banded agate suggested this intarsia portrait to Mr. Heapy. Six pieces of this agate make up the hair. The features are put together in black and white opal with amazing precision considering that the picture below is enlarged from a 1¾ in. by 2¼ in. original.

The art of Cupie Ellis . . . This retired Broken Hill miner, now a White Cliffs opal gouger, has devised and perfected an art form of his own using minerals and gemstones he finds locally. He collects oddly shaped pebbles and crystals which he builds into tableaux, using dendrites in shale or slate as a background, as in the case of the kangaroo and aboriginal boy illustrated. Hollowed rock with glittering inclusions will represent fire in a cave. His stone crosses glitter with gem crystals set in liquid porcelain and one of his religious tableaux already has sold for $200. Mr. Ellis says his biggest problem is to find stones that nature had worked on enough and then use imagination and initiative to expand the idea.

Paul Campbell, president of the Broken Hill Lapidary Group, delights in making useful and beautiful things from petrified wood. He designed a pipe drill on the mud saw principle to make the petrified wood clocks for which he is now locally famous, using a mine waste known as skimps for his abrasive. Below is one of the clocks.

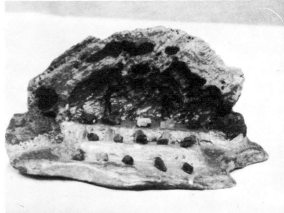

This map of Tasmania was cut from 27 pieces of gemstone by Mr. Alfred Hooper, president of the Lapidary Club of Tasmania, and took 73 hours work. The gemstones, all from different Tasmanian sources, are: 1, petrified wood; 2, opalite; 3, common opal; 4, jasper; 5, jasper; 6, leopard stone (quartz); 7, opalite; 8, chalcedonic serpentine; 9, jasper; 10, jasper; 11, serpentine; 12, jasper; 13, quartzite; 14, agate; 15, petrified wood; 16, petrified wood; 17, jasper; 18, opalite; 19, sanadine porphyry; 20, agatized wood; 21, agate; 22, jasper; 23, beach pebble; 24, agate; 25, jasper; 26, lace agate; 27, agate.

darker yet still bright all go well with their colouring. Eyes and complexion are probably the most important factors in deciding colour. This applies particularly to earrings and necklets, the gemstones of which should complement the eyes while not clashing with the complexion. Grey eyes are the most accommodating and in their case other factors decide the choice of colours.

Most amateur jewellers at one time or another will be asked to design a piece of jewellery to be worn with a particular dress. A general rule in these circumstances is that the jewellery should match or blend with darker materials while setting off lighter dresses. Daring and confidence in the use of contrasts often produce striking results. Simplicity should be the keynote of designs for younger women and girls, although jewellery for the mature woman can be sophisticated and intricately ornamented.

Considerations such as these which dictate the design of jewellery according to its use, class the making of personal jewellery as a decorative art rather than a fine art. Utility is only one of the practical considerations that the designer must bear in mind, however. Settings are subordinate to gemstones in nine cases out of ten and must be designed for the minor role. While remaining unobtrusive, the setting should enhance as well as display the stone.

Clear faceted gems and all transparent or translucent coloured stones require light to show off their beauty. Therefore the first aim of the designer should be to allow as much light as possible to reach the stone by offering the least obstruction to it. Conflicting with this concept of design is the fact that gemstones of this sort are usually costly and the second purpose of the setting is to protect and retain the stone against loss or damage.

The designer must therefore reconcile opposite extremes. His setting must be light without being flimsy, strong and reliable without being oppressive and dull. It must be a prison not only without bars but without high stone walls as well.

With pearls and iridescent gems such as opal and the moonstones or chatoyant tiger-eye, the setting can add to the beauty of the stone by reflection and contrasts of texture. Conversely, the settings of vividly banded, patterned or picture stones such as jaspers, obsidians or agates should be as inconspicuous as possible so that the eye is not drawn from the stone.

Similar rules apply to the combination of various gems in larger pieces of jewellery. Usually the piece will have a central feature, the finest and most costly of the component gems, around which the minor stones are arranged in such a way as to enrich and embellish it. The object of such a design is to lead the eye to the main stone or stones, larger pieces being often designed on a unit system in which a number of similar stones are used in a repetitive pattern.

As far as the amateur jeweller is concerned the combination of gemstones is likely to depend largely upon the nature and quality of material available. More than one or two stones fine enough to justify treatment of this kind are unlikely to be handled at one time.

Most combinations are of coloured stones and waterwhites, the coloured stones generally forming the main feature. Mixing coloured stones is a more perilous undertaking unless the designer studies the principles of colour harmony.

Briefly these are that colours fit into an order of progression from green-yellow to yellow-green through green, blue, purple, red and yellow and that the human eye knows and expects these colours to range from dark to light in a natural sequence with yellow-green, yellow and orange as light colours and blue and purple as dark colours. Clashes as well as pleasing contrasts arise from the pairing of light or dark colours although if the difference in hue is too small the effect may be unpleasant.

Many systems of colour theory have been devised, of which that of the German scientist Wilhelm Ostwald is probably the best known. Ostwald's system is published in the United States as the Color Harmony Manual, a copy of which is of great value to anyone wishing to understand the

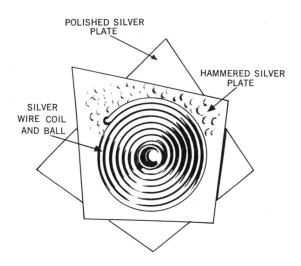

POLISHED SILVER
PLATE

HAMMERED SILVER
PLATE

SILVER
WIRE COIL
AND BALL

*An appliqued free-form brooch or pendant of this type was described in chapter eight.*

mechanics of colour. Few hard and fast rules can be made about colour, however, as it is largely a matter of individual likes and dislikes.

When combining gemstones, the jeweller also often mixes up the cutting styles so that the coloured stone may be seen as a step-cut or cabochon while the waterwhites associated with it are single-cuts or brilliants. This adds variety and interest as well as ensuring that the stones are seen to the best advantage.

Design skills in handmade jewellery are given most scope in articles either made entirely of metal or in which gemstones have a lesser part. It is to these designs that the basic rules of symmetry, proportion and balance apply with most force.

All three qualities share a common meaning while at the same time possessing a slightly different significance. Symmetry, while describing the balancing of the parts of a whole in respect to size, shape or position on opposite sides of an axis, also describes the element of beauty arising from this balance. Artistic balance is defined as harmonious proportion, while proportion is a more geometrical relationship between parts or between parts and a whole.

The combination of all three induces feelings of satisfaction and visual contentment. This combination is usually experienced in the postures and shapes of natural objects, both plant and animal, and often also in the landscape itself. It is this quality, easily understood yet hard to define, that lies at the heart of design. The designer who is able to appreciate it and can embody it in his work stands the best chance of success.

But the jeweller is a craftsman as well as an artist. He must have mastered the medium in which his work is being done before trying to reap the fruits of a flair for design. Otherwise he will be in the position of the painter who never learned to draw. The goal of personal satisfaction and pride of achievement is only attained by the hard road of studying techniques and constant practice.

The amateur artist-craftsman in silver jewellery must first be a proficient silversmith, able to saw and solder, beat and file, so that he or she can unerringly transform an idea into solid shape that is also a living art form.

Practical design also works to rules. It must be consistent with both the material and the processes used to produce the article of jewellery. For instance, the designer who is employing silver as his raw material should avail himself fully of the properties of silver and aim to exploit these properties in the finished article. He should not design for silver as if it was clay or wood. At the same time he should have an ear to the ground for new processes and techniques which his designs can utilise.

Secondly, the design must fit the purpose for which the article is being made. In any object intended for use, the design can never be more important than the article for which it is intended. Often use may give a lead to design. For instance, advantage can be taken of the prominence and exposure to light given to earrings by the use of transparent stones in open settings or plique-a-jour enamels.

Necklaces and bracelets are often composed of arrangements of the same design repeated in various ways. Skilful repetition is one of the most successful gambits in design and offers a rhythmic pleasure to the eye.

Individual devices employed to call attention to a particular part of an object (usually the optical centre) are known as spot designs. Other tricks in the artist-craftsman's repertoire include using lines of varied shapes to induce emotions such as conflict or repose. Lines can also act as a signpost to an important feature of a design.

Forms used in design may be abstract, geometric or obtained from nature. Geometric designs consist of the combination of complete rectangles, triangles or circles or parts of them in agreeable shapes. Abstract designs fall between the formalism of geometric designs and the flowing lines of natural shapes. Nature is the original source of much abstract design as well as the more easily recognised nature motifs.

Nature exists as a vast well of inspiration for the jewellery designer but attempts to copy natural forms too literally result in failure. That someone should be able to copy a flower precisely in silver might be a tribute to his ingenuity and skill as a silversmith. But it would say next to nothing about his talents as an artist and a designer.

The task of the artist whether in paint, stone or metal is not to imitate, but to create. When he designs a rose in silver, his creation should tell the world something about roses and something about silver that has never been told before.

A final word from Mrs. Laurel Gorn, herself one of Australia's jewellery artist-craftsmen. She comments: "The aim of the sincere amateur is to become artist-craftsmen, rather than a jeweller patterned on the tradesman professional, who is in the business to earn his living and is obliged to use all the short cuts he can find.

"This aim requires constant experiment and search for something original. Studying the work of others can be stimulating, but slavish copying is to be deprecated.

"In the days of the Renaissance jewellery was considered one of the arts. A painter or sculptor often worked in the precious metals, notably Cellini, and produced exquisite jewellery. Since then jewellery has degenerated into a trade. It is only very recently, with a growing interest in the craft among amateurs, that exhibitions of the arts throughout the world have included jewellery and the artist-craftsman is fast raising jewellery to its rightful place in the world of art.

"Therefore, new and exciting unconventional pieces are appearing in exhibitions and a growing demand for this type of work is becoming evident.

"It is right that the beginner should learn the fundamentals of the craft and keep to the old and tried conventional methods until he has a thorough grasp of the techniques. Then he should adventure into the wider fields of original, imaginative and creative design.

"Only in this way can jewellery become an art."

# 12

# GEMS IN THE HOME

## By Joseph A. Heapy

WHAT IS THE RIGHT AGE to start gem-carving? Seventy-three, if we take Mr. Joseph A. Heapy, of Waverley, N.S.W., as an example. For that is how old Mr. Heapy was before he carved his first gem seven years ago.

Let us be clear about this. It is not easy to carve gems. It calls for skill and dexterity, tireless concentration and vast stores of patience and enthusiasm. Most hobby gemworkers half Mr. Heapy's age feel gem-carving is too difficult for them to attempt.

The gem-carver needs good eyesight to work on small objects. Mr. Heapy was nearly blind in one eye. But he never stopped to think about his age or whether the work might destroy what little sight he had left. He clipped a 10x double jeweller's loupe over his spectacles and got on with the job.

He was working with fragments of opal so small that he had to use matches as dopsticks. He put together 2,700 of them in one kaleidoscope of colour as the tail of a peacock in one of his finest inlaid jewels.

One feels a temptation to describe this peacock, twinkling in all the blues and yellows, reds and greens of precious opal, as a masterpiece. But it is only one of half-a-dozen pieces of almost equal merit. They represent work of which anyone could be proud. As the work of a man in the years between 73 and 80, they are nothing short of phenomenal.

Mr. Heapy encourages his friends and fellow members of the Lapidary Club of New South Wales to take his jewel miniatures for granted. He does not think it amazing that a man his age who has only one good eye should be able to do work of this calibre. He prefers people merely to see his miniatures as works of art, extensions by human skill of the natural beauty of gemstones.

He would rather encourage other people to emulate his feats than tell of the difficulty and hardship they cost him. Best of all he likes to describe methods and techniques that he discovered by trial and error.

Mr. Heapy's story began 21 years ago when he won $10,000 in a lottery and decided to retire. "I needed a hobby to fill my spare time, one in which I could give expression to my feelings and the wish to create something original and lasting," he told me. "Gemstones, particularly opal, fascinated me."

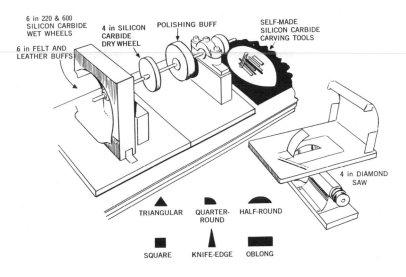

*The simple tools with which Mr Joseph Heapy has carved his gem masterpieces. Shown are the shapes of the tools he has made for himself from a fine-grained block of silicon carbide.*

He bought some machinery—a double-headed arbor, a 6 in. diamond saw, a diamond lap, three 6 in. felt buffs, two silicon carbide wheels, emery cloth, pumice and rouge—and cut his first cabochons. "These being large enough, I held them in my fingers. I had never heard of a dopstick." A trip to Lightning Ridge gained him half a sugar bag of opal fragments for $10.

Eventually he tired of cutting cabochons and faceting. It was "a mass of repetitive work. I decided to find something new and different . . ." He decided to try gem inlays and bought a dentist's drill but could find no diamond tipped tools. "Having a few diamond crystals by me, I crushed them into splinters and soldered these on the shanks of dental burrs to use with the flexible arm."

*Tumbled chips of garnet, amethyst, amazonite, rhodocrosite, blue quartz and carnelian were used by Mrs Betty Kerslake of Artarmon, NSW, to make this picture in gems. Green aventurine made the leaves with 20 gauge 9 carat gold wire as the stems. The bow is a bought jewellers' finding and the plastic frame is also bought.*

Taking a piece of black opal potch, he cut gutters and drilled holes to inlay a geometric pattern with pieces of opal. The inlay was one-thirty-second of an inch thick and it was covered with a layer of rock crystal for protection. This rock crystal, flawlessly ground and polished to about one-sixteenth of an inch thick on a marble slab, covers all his pieces.

Getting rid of air bubbles in the epoxy cement is quite a problem. Methylated spirit cleans the cement off both rock crystal and fingers. Both cover and piece must be warmed until they are almost too hot to handle to clear the cement. Any remaining bubbles are carefully squeezed out as the crystal is slid over the inlay or intarsia.

In his next inlay—a butterfly—Mr. Heapy introduced gold wire rolled into a thin ribbon and set on edge. A flower pendant (often worn by his late wife), a bird and a moth followed and finally the magnificent peacock, the iridescent tail feathers of which rise on individual strands of gold.

By this time inlay was proving too tedious and exacting. Mr. Heapy went on to intarsia without ever as much as having heard the word before. He sketched a seascape on paper and then created it in a jigsaw of gemstone fragments. A yacht of agate with white opal sails approaches a shore of opal matrix through an opal sea and beneath an agate sky.

Mr. Heapy cuts his paper sketches into their component parts and sticks each piece to a tiny slab of the appropriate gem material, each one-sixteenth of an inch thick. Shaping is done on a 4 in. diamond saw.

"This is the most important part," he said. "Take the piece between the thumb and forefinger of each hand. Come down on the blade gently and feather it left and right, making the movement light and slow.

"Do not try to remove too much material at a time or you may make the saw grab and shatter the stone. I remove no more than a few thousandths of an inch at a time. Small curves and hollows are cut easily, using care."

Large curves are cut on the edge of an 8 in. silicon carbide wheel and awkward angles and corners with small silicon carbide hand tools which Mr. Heapy makes to suit each task in hand. "Make sure you keep the sides of each piece square with the face," he advises. "If you undercut or have them irregular in any way the joins will show."

First the picture is assembled on a piece of cardboard to ensure that every detail is perfect. The final picture is built up with cement on a plate of nickel silver cut to size. "Select what you consider the key piece —which could be a corner or middle piece—and cement that in place first, leaving it to set overnight. If you set the lot down at once some of the pieces may wander, showing gaps."

The cemented picture is ground flat on marble or plate glass with 220 and 500 grit and water ("I use a straight-edge from time to time to make sure it is flat") then sanded and polished before covering with rock crystal.

A succession of gem pictures were produced by these methods. A fine Egyptian head, flashing in blues and reds and outlined in gold, then a white opal sunbather on a beach of opal matrix and obsidian. A fragment of white opal suffused with fire became the body of She, the goddess of Rider Haggard's book, bathing in flame to become immortal.

Gem material now suggests subjects to Mr. Heapy. Another brilliant opal fragment became the mouth of a volcano belching fire. On this gem picture he used a new and even more painstaking technique, breaking up the colour masses into sections. "By this means, I control light and shade, giving better contrasts and strengthening my foregrounds."

A piece of agate suggested "waves breaking on golden sands" and a tropical island scene resulted. Another fragment of agate with wavy lines of cream and reddish-brown like the lights on a woman's hair started Mr. Heapy on his first full-face portrait.

"The delicacy of light and shade for the hair and face required picking just the right pieces," he said. "The eyes, nose and mouth had to be inlaid, using very small pieces of the right shades to get the true expression of life. This required more concentration than any of my previous intarsias."

For a break from the strain of intarsia, Mr. Heapy carves alunite, the greyish, pinkish waxy-looking sulphate of potassium and aluminium. One of the best of these charming little productions he calls Maid with a Hoop.

He incorporated a mirror as a backing in another alunite carving which he calls the God of Gems. This is a herculean figure holding up a cabochon of transparent red-brown obsidian.

Alunite is one of the materials favoured by another Sydney gem-carver, Ross Fraser of Burwood. Mr. Fraser, who collects most of the material he carves, fashioned a piece of pink alunite he found near Buladelah, N.S.W., into a mouse. This mouse has eyes of carnelian and ears of prehnite.

Mr. Fraser is another gifted amateur who has never had an art lesson. However, compared to Mr. Heapy he is only a youngster. Mr. Fraser was 55 when he took up carving three years ago. Like Mr. Heapy he wanted to get away from cutting cabochons.

Without intending any pun on the bunch of grapes that is one of his masterpieces, Mr. Fraser carves in the round. The bunch of grapes was his first carving project with leaves shaped from mottled green Tasmanian serpentine and twig-thin stalks of red-brown jasper.

Mr. Fraser sliced amethyst crystals from Broken Hill into cubes and rounded each one into a grape by hand on his 10 in. grinding wheel. The result was a picture in every sense of the word. Later it was joined by a spray of agate daisies as a companion piece.

One of the finest things Mr. Fraser has done is a flower so delicate that it is hard to believe gemstones yielded the beautifully marked prehnite petals or the stalks and leaves of Queensland chrysoprase. Almost as captivating as the prehnite flower is a rose of Broken Hill rhodocrosite with stalks and leaves of green jasper.

Mr. Fraser and his wife Mavis are founder members of Sydney's Western suburbs Lapidary Club. In May, 1966, they made a 20-week tour of 7,000 miles to see Queensland and Northern Territory gemfields.

His work includes a Skye terrier carved from an 8 in. block of green jasper, a swan in yellow quartz, birds in smoky quartz and chert, a penguin in black and white jasper. The Frasers' home is filled with lovely things that are also souvenirs of happy outings.

Like most gem-carvers Mr. Fraser has had to devise his own tools and techniques to a large extent. Ideas came easily for he was a tool-maker by trade. He has shaped boxwood wheels for cutting into narrow spaces and hard felts for polishing but he tries to get rid of most of the waste material with his diamond saw.

The fascination of shaping and polishing gemstones has spread all over Australia. One of the people who finds satisfaction and pleasure in the gem riches of Broken Hill is former miner and White Cliffs opal gouger Bill Ellis, known to his friends as Cupie.

He is locally famous for the murals, figurines and religious grottoes he has made with local stones and crystals. Allan Ireland, who told me about Mr. Ellis, added: "He says the biggest job is to find the stones that nature has worked hard enough on and then to use initiative and imagination to expand the idea."

In the cheery Broken Hill way, Paul Campbell, president of the lapidary club, gets called by the name of a firm of local wood merchants. The reason? He is so fond of working with petrified wood.

A miner at North Mine, he has devised what might be called a mud drill using waste from the mines as an abrasive to bore petrified wood by the mud saw method. Into the hole thus drilled in a brilliantly polished block of petrified wood he fits a clock. A local policeman was presented with one of Paul's clocks on his transfer to Glen Innes.

*This delightful picture in opal, prase, obsidian and tiger-eye, mounted on burgundy velvet, represents many months' work by Mr and Mrs Lloyd Meller, of Epping, NSW.*

Every gem hobbyist sooner or later has something of beauty in his home, even if it is only a jewelled sugar-spoon or a penstand mounted on a brilliant slab of agate.

To some the gem hobby has brought beautiful and precious possessions. Everyone entering Lloyd Meller's home at Epping, N.S.W., is delighted by the opal flower-pot picture that kept Lloyd and his wife Peggy busy for a year.

The obsidian flower-pot was flat-lapped by hand on a sheet of plate glass with 400 and 600 grits before being polished. A total of 62 opals in shades of white and blue make up the flowers. Leaves and stalks are

Mrs F. M. Hooper of Blackman's Bay, Tasmania, succeeded in carving this paper knife entirely from three pieces of New Zealand greenstone which made the hilt, crossbar and blade.

This butterknife has a handle of nephrite jade. Mr J. R. Fuller of the Tasmanian Lapidary Club cut the blade from brass plate which was later silverplated.

J. R. Tuffley of the Lapidary Club of Tasmania carved an agate handle to fit this cocktail fork.

Tumbled gemstones made this turtle for Mrs Madge Hitchcock of Hobart, Tasmania.

Mrs Stella Burns, of Claremont, Tasmania, carved this butterfly from gemstones she found near her home. The wings are of petrified wood and the body of common opal.

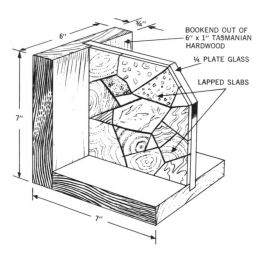

BOOKEND OUT OF 6" x 1" TASMANIAN HARDWOOD

¼ PLATE GLASS

LAPPED SLABS

The method by which Mr B. Goldsmith of the Tasmanian Lapidary Society made these attractive intarsia bookends is described in the text.

prase and a bee, added for effect, has a body of tiger-eye. The whole is mounted in a frame on a background of burgundy velvet.

Rating high among gemstone lovers are the Lapidary Club of Tasmania. Illustrations accompanying this chapter prove the enthusiasm of this group whose president, Mr. Alfred Hooper, sets the standard with his remarkable map of Tasmania in 27 slabs of gemstone, shown on another page.

One of the most novel and interesting of the Tasmanian designs are Mr. B. Goldsmith's intarsia bookends. These were made from six by one inch pieces of Tasmanian oak rebated for glass, glued and screwed together and French polished.

Slabs of banded and fortification agates, plume agates, orbicular jasper, onyx, obsidian and petrified woods were individually lapped, polished and fitted.

The edges of the slabs were cemented together and laid face down on a sheet of waste glass covered with waxed paper and weighted with another sheet of glass on waxed paper.

After being allowed to set for three or four days, the entire intarsia was cemented on quarter-inch plate glass. After again being allowed to set, this was fitted and secured into the rebate of the timber with waterproof glue. The bottom of each bookend was covered with felt.

The result is a gemstone novelty anyone would be proud to own.

## COSTS

Carving tools—Flexible drive unit, with foot control, $45.90; flexible drive shaft, $11; bench grinder/polisher with flexible shaft, 1/6 h.p., $56.10; diamond wheel, $7.96; diamond point, $6.15; drum sander, $1.15.

Cratex points, 8c to 12c; point mandrel, 25c; wheels, 8c-12c; wheel mandrel, 60c; silicon carbide points, 60 and 80 grit, 40c-55c; felt buffs, 60c.

These prices, current at the end of 1966, are subject to fluctuation and are not binding on any lapidary dealer.

# APPENDIX

Public facilities for instruction in lapidary and jewellery-making throughout Australia are:

## NEW SOUTH WALES:

1,151 pupils enrolled at 76 lapidary classes and 461 at 32 jewellery-making classes. Classes are held at the following evening colleges (figures for jewellery-making in brackets):

> *Ashfield*, 3 classes (3 classes) 46 pupils (48 pupils); *Avalon*, 4 (3) 52 (35); *Bankstown*, 2 (nil) 42; *Bondi*, 2 (1) 30 (16); *Broken Hill*, 2 (nil) 20; *Burwood*, 3 (2) 49 (33); *Campsie*, 3 (1) 42 (14); *Canberra*, 2 (nil) 42; *Cardiff*, 1 (nil) 14; *Chatswood*, 2 (4) 38 (56); *Eastwood*, 5 (1) 86 (15); *Fairfield*, 5 (2) 83 (31); *Hamilton*, 2 (nil) 36; *Hornsby*, 4 (1) 61 (19); *Hurstville*, 2 (1) 23 (13); *Kogarah*, 5 (2) 68 (23); *Leichhardt*, 1 (nil) 10; *Manly*, 2 (nil) 28; *Maroubra*, 2 (nil) 20; *Mosman*, 2 (2) 37 (32); *Macquarie*, 4 (1) 45 (16); *Narrabeen*, 2 (1) 32 (11); *North Ryde*, 2 (nil) 28; *Parramatta*, 2 (2) 42 (36); *Penrith*, 2 (1) 30 (15); *Riverstone*, 2 (nil) 26; *St. Marys*, 1 (1) 18 (10); *Springwood*, 1 (nil) 14; *Sutherland*, 4 (2) 65 (25); *Westmead*, 2 (1) 24 (13).

Fees of $4 a term entitle the student to all the facilities of the college and may be paid at 40 cents a week if desired. Evening Colleges are run by the Department of Education, G.P.O. Box No. 33, Sydney.

## QUEENSLAND:

The Board of Adult Education provides classes in Brisbane, Maryborough and other places from time to time in geology and mineralogy which are free. It does not usually conduct stone-cutting or polishing classes but lapidary groups exist which do so. The Board's address is Adult Education Centre, c/o Parliament House Post Office, Brisbane.

## SOUTH AUSTRALIA:

The Adult Education Service of the Education Department conducts classes in lapidary and copper jewellery at these adult education centres:

> *Croydon Boys' Technical High School,* West Croydon; *Goodwood Boys' Tech. H.S.,* Goodwood; *Le Fevre Boys' Tech. H.S.,* Semaphore; *Mitcham Girls' Tech. H.S.* (3 classes), Kingswood; *Norwood Boys' Tech. H.S.,* Marryatville; *Strathmont Boys' Tech. H.S.,* Gilles Plains; *Vermont Girls' Tech. H.S.,* South Plympton. Copper jewellery-making classes are held at *Eyre Peninsula Adult Education Centre,* Box 562, Port Lincoln; *Murray Bridge A.E.C.,* Swanport Road, Murray Bridge; *Onkaparinga A.E.C.,* Box 78, Mount Barker.

A total of 135 students enrolled, paying $5 a term for two-hour classes, $5.50 for $2\frac{1}{2}$ hours. During the past 18 months an upsurge of interest in jewellery-making took place. Classes are run by the Education Department, G.P.O. Box 406c, Adelaide.

## TASMANIA:

The Adult Education Board has done a little lapidary work at its Art Summer School and in one country centre at Burnie. It is hoped to help groups at other country centres. The Board's addresses are 16 Argyle Street, Hobart, and 452 Elizabeth Street, North Hobart.

## VICTORIA:

Instruction in jewellery-making for part-time hobby students is offered at:

> *Royal Melbourne Institute of Technology,* 124 Latrobe Street, Melbourne, C.1., *Caulfield Technical College,* 900 Dandenong Road, East Caulfield, Melbourne, S.E.5, and *Prahran Technical College,* 142 High Street, Prahran, Melbourne, S.1.

They are run by the Technical Schools Division of the State Education Department, Treasury Place, Melbourne, C.2.

## WESTERN AUSTRALIA:

The University of Western Australia Adult Education Board started a class in jewellery-making on 20th September, 1966, at Kent Street High School, Perth. The instructor, Sydney-trained artist and art teacher Geoff Allen wrote: "I intend to introduce each phase of the work, i.e. soldering, sawing, forming, chain-making, colouring, polishing, etc., throughout the twelve lessons. I hope also to stimulate creative thinking in design . . ." The class was limited to 18 with a fee of $9. The Board's address is 3 Howard Street, Perth.

## BIRTHDAY STONES

January, *garnet*; February, *amethyst*; March, *aquamarine* (alternative bloodstone); April, *diamond* (rock crystal); May, *emerald* (chryso-prase); June, *pearl* (moonstone); July, *ruby* (carnelian); August, *peridot* (sardonyx); September, *sapphire* (lapis lazuli); October, *opal*; November, *topaz*; December, *turquoise*.

This list is issued by the National Association of Goldsmiths, the organisation representing British jewellers. The list issued by the American National Retail Jewellers Association makes bloodstone the first choice for March, sardonyx the first choice for August and tourmaline, yellow quartz and zircon alternatives for October, November and December respectively.

## GAUGES FOR SILVER WIRE AND SHEET

In Australia silver wire and sheet are produced in Standard Wire Gauges (S.W.G.). In the United States, Brown & Sharp (B. & S.) gauges are used and this fact should be borne in mind when working to American data.

| S.W.G. | Diameter in inches | Nearest B. & S. | Diameter in inches |
|---|---|---|---|
| 10 | .128 | 8 | .1285 |
| 11 | .116 | 9 | .1144 |
| 12 | .104 | 10 | .1019 |
| 13 | .092 | 11 | .0907 |
| 14 | .080 | 12 | .0808 |
| 15 | .072 | 13 | .0720 |
| 16 | .064 | 14 | .0641 |
| 17 | .056 | 15 | .0571 |
| 18 | .048 | 16 | .0508 |
|  |  | 17 | .0453 |
| 19 | .040 | 18 | .0403 |
| 20 | .036 | 19 | .0359 |
| 21 | .032 | 20 | .0320 |
| 22 | .028 | 21 | .0285 |
| 23 | .024 | 22 | .0253 |
| 24 | .022 | 23 | .0226 |
| 25 | .020 | 24 | .0201 |
| 26 | .018 | 25 | .0179 |
| 27 | .0164 | 26 | .0159 |
| 28 | .0148 | 27 | .0142 |
| 29 | .0136 |  |  |
| 30 | .0124 | 28 | .0126 |
| 31 | .0116 |  |  |
| 32 | .0108 | 29 | .0113 |
| 33 | .0100 | 30 | .0100 |
| 34 | .0092 | 31 | .0089 |
| 35 | .0084 | 32 | .0079 |
| 36 | .0076 | 33 | .0078 |

| S.W.G. | Diameter in inches | Nearest B. & S. | Diameter in inches |
|--------|--------------------|------------------|--------------------|
| 37 | .0068 | 34 | .0063 |
| 38 | .0060 | 35 | .0056 |
| 39 | .0052 | 36 | .0050 |
| 40 | .0048 | 37 | .0044 |
| 41 | .0044 | — | — |
| 42 | .0040 | 38 | .0039 |
| 43 | .0035 | 39 | .0035 |
| 44 | .0030 | 40 | .0031 |
| 45 | .0028 | — | — |
| 46 | .0025 | — | — |
| 47 | .0020 | — | — |
| 48 | .0016 | — | — |
| 49 | .0012 | — | — |
| 50 | .0010 | — | — |

If an exact thickness is important the equivalent in inches should be quoted rather than the gauge number.

It is advisable to standardise on even S.W.G. gauges (i.e. 12, 14, 16 S.W.G., etc.) as these are always available from stock and selling prices are based on bulk production. An intermediate gauge (13, 15, 17 S.W.G., etc.) usually entails a delay and unless a large quantity is involved, may be as expensive per foot or per square inch as the next heavier gauge.

SQUARE WIRES: Square silver wires are readily available from stock in 12, 14, 16, 18, 19 and 20 S.W.G. It should be borne in mind that a square wire is "bigger" (i.e. heavier per foot) than the same gauge in round wire. In round figures 14 S.W.G. square would be as heavy as 13 S.W.G. round; 16 S.W.G. square is equal to 15 S.W.G. round and so on.

GAUGES FOR COPPER AND PEWTER: Exactly the same position regarding gauges, mentioned above, applies to both copper and pewter, i.e. S.W.G. gauges are used in Australia and B. & S. gauges in the United States. Therefore the above tables, although headed silver, will also apply for copper wire and sheet and for pewter sheet.

(Gauges and other data supplied by the Precious Metal Refining Co. of Sydney, and Mrs. Doris Thompson of the Australian Silvercraft Centre, Sydney.)

# INDEX

Printed by The Continental Printing Company
Limited, Hong Kong